THE UNOFFICIAL DIVERGENT APTITUDE TEST

DISCOVER YOUR TRUE FACTION!

Noel St. Clair

This book is unofficial and unauthorized. It is not approved, licensed, or endorsed by Veronica Roth, her publishers, Lions Gate Entertainment Corporation, or any affiliated or associated company.

Avon, Massachusetts

Copyright © 2015 by F+W Media, Inc.
All rights reserved.
This book, or parts thereof, may not be reproduced in any form without permission from the publisher; exceptions are made for brief excerpts used in published reviews.

Published by
Adams Media, a division of F+W Media, Inc.
57 Littlefield Street, Avon, MA 02322. U.S.A.
www.adamsmedia.com

ISBN 10: 1-4405-8514-8
ISBN 13: 978-1-4405-8514-2
eISBN 10: 1-4405-8515-6
eISBN 13: 978-1-4405-8515-9

Printed by RR Donnelley, Harrisonburg, VA, U.S.A.

10 9 8 7 6 5 4 3 2 1

January 2015

Library of Congress Cataloging-in-Publication Data

St. Clair, Noel.
  The unofficial divergent aptitude test / Noel St. Clair.
    pages cm
  ISBN 978-1-4405-8514-2 (pb) -- ISBN 1-4405-8514-8 (pb) -- ISBN 978-1-4405-8515-9 (ebook) -- ISBN 1-4405-8515-6 (ebook)
  1. Personality tests--Juvenile literature. 2. Occupational aptitude tests--Juvenile literature. 3. Interest inventories--Juvenile literature. 4. Personality and occupation--Juvenile literature. I. Title.
  BF698.5.S72 2015
  153.9'4--dc23
                                       2014045488

This book is unofficial and unauthorized. It is not approved, licensed, or endorsed by Veronica Roth, her publishers, Lions Gate Entertainment Corporation, or any affiliated or associated company.

Many of the designations used by manufacturers and sellers to distinguish their products are claimed as trademarks. Where those designations appear in this book and F+W Media, Inc. was aware of a trademark claim, the designations have been printed with initial capital letters.

Cover design by Jessica Pooler.
Cover images © Clipart.com; Anastasiia Sochyvets/seamartini/Svetlana Chernyavsky/anthonycz/Pongson Chingchoo/Gui Yongnian/123RF; iStockphoto.com/ambassador806/by_adr.

This book is available at quantity discounts for bulk purchases.
For information, please call 1-800-289-0963.

CONTENTS

Introduction 5

How to Use This Book 7

Part 1: The Quizzes 9

Part 2: Discover Your Faction 165
    Faction Breakdown 1: Abnegation 166
    Faction Breakdown 2: Amity 173
    Faction Breakdown 3: Candor 180
    Faction Breakdown 4: Dauntless 187
    Faction Breakdown 5: Erudite 193
    Faction Breakdown 6: Divergent 200

Afterword 207

INTRODUCTION

This book will transport you to a world very unlike our own. A place where peace (supposedly) reigns. A society that functions due to the cooperation of five factions, each filled with people who share a particular set of values.

A world in which, rather than choosing your own fate, your fate chooses you.

If you're unfamiliar with the universe of the Divergent series—or simply need a refresher—here's how it works: At age sixteen, each member of this postapocalyptic society takes an aptitude test, during which one's reactions to virtual situations reveal one's true nature. From this test, each persons result is labeled as one of society's five factions: Abnegation (for the selfless), Amity (for the diplomatic), Candor (for the honest), Dauntless (for the courageous), and Erudite (for the wise).

Upon receiving these official outcomes, it's up to each person to choose her faction wisely after careful contemplation; after all, it is within these groups that she will spend the rest of her life.

Now, for most people, determining a faction is easy and clear-cut. For others, like Beatrice (Tris) Prior, choosing just a single path is a struggle. And these individuals have their own designation, though it's best not to say it out loud.

Divergent.

Within these pages, you will be able to see what it might be like to be a part of the Divergent universe and discover which faction best fits you.

But not to worry; there won't be any electrodes you'll need to be hooked up to, no vial of serum to drink, and no scary simulations to watch. And, unlike in the Divergent series, it's completely okay to tell other people your results, even if they're inconclusive. (Best part: There also aren't consequences for being factionless. *Whew.*)

Think of this book like your own personal Choosing Ceremony—without, you know, that whole "having to adhere to one way of life for the rest of your days, or else" thing.

HOW TO USE THIS BOOK

This aptitude test is divided into two parts. Part 1 takes you through a series of fifty "What you would do?" quizzes, ultimately leading you to discover your ideal faction.

Rather than having to choose between two items—say, a piece of cheese and a knife, as Beatrice did in her aptitude test—you'll discover your faction (or whether you're Divergent, like Tris) by deciding how you might react to given scenarios. Do you thirst for knowledge, like Caleb does? Do you crave daredevil activities, like Uriah? These quizzes will reveal the answers to these questions, and many more.

Part 2 breaks each faction down so you can learn more about how your faction relates to your life in today's world. (No initiation required!) Here you'll gain valuable insights into your personality, your activities and hobbies, your personal style, your love life, your friendships, and more!

Use this book however it best suits you. You can take these quizzes on your own, or share this book with a friend to discover your paths together. You could even involve your whole family and stage your own at-home Choosing Ceremony. So, get creative!

And now it's time for your Aptitude Test to begin. Will Abnegation, Amity, Candor, Dauntless, or Erudite be the ideal faction for you? Or will you be . . . Divergent?

PART 1

THE QUIZZES

Before you begin your Aptitude Test, you should take heed of a couple key points in preparation. The fifty questions found in Part 1 will outline various scenarios. Some are situations that you may have experienced in your own life. Some are events that you'll probably experience in the future. And some are hypothetical circumstances that you have likely never experienced—and perhaps never will. Each question has six possible outcomes, and it is your task to choose one—and only one—answer for each question.

The way you answer the majority of the questions will determine which faction you end up in: Abnegation, Amity, Candor, Dauntless, or Erudite. If your answers don't place you in any of these factions, you're Divergent. As you answer, keep in mind that, most likely, the answer choices will not offer an option that describes *exactly* what you would do in a given circumstance. If this is the case, just do your best to provide the answer that's closest to what you would actually do if you found yourself in that situation.

After you finish your test, you'll find a chart in the Scoring section at the end of Part 1 that will help you determine your faction. For now, simply answer each question truthfully and to the best of your ability.

Without further ado, your test awaits. Good luck.

QUIZ #1

THE WOMAN ON THE STREET

It's nighttime, and you're walking home after having dinner with some of your friends. You pull your coat tightly around you to combat a chill breeze that's nearly making you shiver. You wonder if it may even start to rain, given how cold it's getting, but you look up at the sky and see that there are no clouds, just a smattering of tiny stars.

As you round the next corner, you see a homeless woman huddled on the sidewalk in the distance—you see that she's wearing nothing but a T-shirt and jeans. As you get closer, you see that she has a skinny dog with her and she's sitting on the ground, counting pennies she's received from other passersby out of a dirtied Styrofoam cup. Her face is lined and weathered, likely from living outside and never being shielded from the elements of sun and wind. Her feet are bare, save for some thin socks. If she's not cold already, she will be as the night continues to cool.

She bears no sign asking for help, and doesn't even seem to really notice you as you approach. She's not looking for a handout, or even a kind word. She just continues to count her change.

What do you do?

A. You crouch down next to her and give her some change, and talk with her for a while before saying goodbye with a hug.

B. You give her your coat and your shoes—you only have ten more blocks to walk until you get home—as well as the last of the money from your wallet, so she can get something to eat.

C. You give her some cash and your scarf.

D. You would give her your coat, but you just bought it after saving up for a whole year—so you tell her that before giving her a couple of dollars.

E. You pop into the local fast food joint and buy her a meal and a coffee—food will keep her strong.

F. You try to be helpful. You ask if she knows where the nearest homeless shelter is so she can get out of the cold, and you provide her with directions if needed.

QUIZ #2

THE BEACH PANIC

You're enjoying a day at the beach with all of your friends. You've spent hours swimming, lying on your towel in the sand (trying to catch a bit of a tan, to be honest), and just hanging out. So far, it's been perfect. Right now you're reading a magazine, soaking in the last hour or so of your time near the shore.

Then, out in the water, you hear screaming. At first you think it's just some kids messing around, so you continue reading. But then other people start shouting. There's a crowd at the edge of the surf looking out to sea. You and your friends stand up to get a better look and you see a tiny head with arms flailing. Someone is drowning. It looks like a little kid out there.

You look toward the lifeguard station and don't see anything or anyone. You turn back to the ocean; no one has jumped in to try to rescue the boy or girl. It appears that there's a huge swell pushing the child farther out—if someone goes out there alone, he or she might drown, too, rather than save the kid. It's a very risky move to try to swim to the child.

What do you do?

A. Brainstorm a plan: You see if anyone in the vicinity has a kayak or canoe—this way, one or a few of you can go out there and save the child without drowning yourselves.

B. You call 911—to be honest, you're not sure that the child will survive and you want to make sure the ambulance is there ASAP.

C. Jump in the water without thinking and swim as fast as you can to get to the child, no matter what the risk.

D. Go with a group of people who volunteer to swim out to save the child. Hopefully at least one of you will make it back safely with him or her in tow.

E. Try to locate the child's parents (or whoever brought the kid to the beach).

F. Watch as someone else jumps in to save the child, then gather the group of onlookers for a nondenominational prayer circle.

QUIZ #3

THE BANK ROBBERY

It's 9 A.M., and you're at the bank right when it opens so you can deposit some cash you made from your afterschool job. There's already quite a long line, so you settle into it and pull out your cell phone to browse Instagram while you wait.

Suddenly, a man whips by you, knocking your shoulder, then jumps onto the teller's desk and begins to yell. He's got a gun. Yes, this is robbery. And you are terrified.

He commands everyone to put their hands up, then slowly drop to the floor. You see people around you in slow motion, raising their arms then dropping to their knees. In the split second you have before you follow suit, you weigh your options. There's a door pretty close to you—you wonder if you have time to burst out of line and through the doors before the guy notices you.

Then the bank goes into lockdown mode: Gates are closing automatically over the doors, over the windows, over every single possible escape route. Someone in the back must have pulled the alarm. You're definitely trapped. And the robber is livid.

You put your hands in the air and start lowering yourself to the bank's gray and white marble floor, your mind racing. The robber is busy stuffing cash from the tellers' stations into a black canvas bag, every so often brandishing his gun at the crowd to keep people still.

When he finishes, he asks people one by one to move to another area of the room so he can continue his quest for cash, and, presumably, escape.

What do you do?

A. Stay alert—and protect the others around you—without calling any attention to yourself.

B. Comply immediately with the robber's requests without questioning them.

C. Shield others around you and slide your wallet to the robber without being asked, just in case it might help.

D. Attack the robber and wrestle him to the ground until help arrives.

E. Play dead—this way, no one notices you and you have the best chance of making it out alive.

F. Use your cell phone to covertly call 911—letting a bad guy get away with his plan is completely unjust.

QUIZ #4

THE DINNER PARTY

It's Saturday night and, as per usual, you're at a friend's house having a couples dinner party. Typically the evening includes a nice meal, maybe a game or two, and some fun conversation—it's a chance for everyone to hang out and relax with each other. (And way cheaper than going out to dinner, that's for sure!)

The couple who hosts usually spends the whole day planning and prepping, which means they always seem a bit tired once everyone arrives (and the female of the couple more so—it always seems that the women put more time into planning these nights than the men do).

You sit down for an amazing meal. Your friend's been pulling recipes off Pinterest and went all out this week, cooking filet mignon, roasted vegetables, and potatoes au gratin. Everyone is having a great time laughing and catching up.

The meal is winding down and the hostess gets up to clear the dishes. A couple of people help her and then everyone settles back down in their seats, anticipating some hang out time before dessert.

What are you most likely to do right now?

A. Lead the group in a discussion of politics and current events—you love the chance to pick people's brains.

B. Put on some music or start playing around on the piano to give the evening some ambiance.

C. Ask the men to do the dishes—pointing out that it's typically the women who prep and cook for these events anyway.

D. Suggest a game to take the evening up a notch—you're always ready for some friendly competition.

E. Tell the hostess you'll help her wash the dishes later, then lead her back to the living room so you can all hang out together.

F. Busy yourself in the kitchen cleaning the dishes. The hostess shouldn't have to do the washing up after having everyone over and cooking.

QUIZ #5

THE LUNCH ROOM TAKE-DOWN

It's lunchtime at school, and everyone is gathered around tables or waiting in line to buy food in the cafeteria. It's mostly upperclassmen at this lunch period, but there are a couple of younger students, too, mostly those in the gifted or accelerated program who take upperclass classes.

There's a particularly nerdy boy in the lunch line, waiting to purchase his meal. Suddenly, a big older boy who's a known troublemaker confronts him and demands his lunch money. The younger boy protests at first, exclaiming that if he doesn't have any money, he won't be able to eat his lunch.

The older boy doesn't care. He keeps pestering the boy. The younger boy tries to ignore him, squinting his eyes to pretend to read the menu over the older boy's head. This only angers the older boy more. He shoves the younger boy to the ground and pries the money out of his grasp. The younger boy yelps in protest but relinquishes the crumpled up dollars. He knows he won't be able to win this fight. The older boy takes the younger boy's place in line, and no one says anything about it. The younger boy begins limping toward the cafeteria door.

You're watching all of this from your seat at a table with your friends. No one has approached the younger boy to even ask if he's okay.

What do you do?

A. Confront the thief and give him a piece of your mind ... and fist, if necessary.

B. Wait until the thief leaves, then comfort the boy and offer to share your lunch with him.

C. Go find a teacher and tell him what happened, giving a full, unbiased account of who was at fault.

D. Not wanting to anger the thief (or make yourself a target), you stay out of it. You make a mental note to never anger that older boy.

E. Give the boy your lunch money so he doesn't go hungry. You'll be fine.

F. You ask everyone at your table to spare some change or a dollar, then give the kid the cash you collected so he can buy lunch.

QUIZ #6

THE PUBLIC KISS

It's Saturday night, and you and your friends are hanging out at the local mall waiting to catch a movie. You're laughing and talking in the food court while grabbing a quick bite to eat before the show.

You're in the middle of a story about your history teacher and his crazy in-class antics when one of your friends starts laughing and pointing at something behind you. Over on a bench against the food court wall, there's a couple that's probably just around your age totally making out. Really, people? Really?!

Your entire table turns for a minute to gape at this duo, who seem completely unaware that they're in public—in a super crowded public gathering place, at that—and that there are probably about a hundred people staring at them at this point, many of whom are kids and families. They truly have not a care or thought in the world, save for each other. Which, you guess, must be nice.

What's your reaction to this scene?

A. Feel totally awkward and avert your eyes.

B. Glare at them. Who do they think they are?!

C. Feel happy for them—love is a wonderful thing—but you don't want to embarrass them by staring too much.

D. Let out a long, loud whistle in their direction, causing them to stop making out and stare at you. Then you wink at them.

E. Walk up to them and tell them that their behavior is totally inappropriate—there are tons of kids here. Get. A. Room.

F. Study their behavior as if the sight were an animal mating ritual that you'd like to better understand.

QUIZ #7

THE HOT-HEADED BOSS

You work at an advertising agency, and you and your team just finished pitching a proposal to a brand-new client. This client would bring in a ton of money to your company—and to your pockets—if the campaign gets picked up and succeeds as anticipated.

However, the client, while impressed with your ideas, says his company wants to go in a different direction and is going to choose another agency. He excuses himself from the meeting, leaving you, your team, and your boss in the room.

Suddenly your boss goes on a crazy rant, pointing fingers at you and members of the team and naming random reasons why the client didn't choose your agency. She's completely unfounded and seems to just be blowing off a lot of hot air—something she does regularly when a pitch doesn't go your way.

You can tell that her yelling is making everyone feel uncomfortable and deflated. You all worked your hearts out on this campaign and you all really wanted to land this client—you worked nights and weekends to get everything perfect. So, not only is your boss in the wrong here, but she's making everyone feel like there's no point in working so hard since it doesn't mean anything to her in the end. Sure, you didn't get the client, but that's part of life. You can't win over them all.

She's still yelling. What do you do?

A. Try to figure out an alternate client while she yells so that you can be ready with a suggestion by the time she's done.

B. Raise your hand to interject and calmly say that her yelling is not going to motivate you and the team to move past this setback.

C. Interrupt your boss and, at equal voice volume, tell her she's being completely unreasonable and unprofessional.

D. Stare at your hands on the conference room table, feeling totally uncomfortable.

E. Excuse yourself from the room. You're super angry at her reaction and don't want to blow up.

F. Wait patiently until her rant is over, then ask if there is anything you can do to help fix this situation.

QUIZ #8

THE GRAND-MOTHER AT THE GROCERY STORE

You're having some friends over for dinner tonight, so you pop over to the grocery store after work to grab a couple of items for the meal. You're in a bit of a time crunch, so you walk quickly through the aisles and manage to get what you need and check out in five minutes flat. Whew!

Hustling through the parking lot with your groceries, you don't even see the car pulling out just ahead of you—that is, until the back of it strikes the front of your cart, knocking you almost to the ground. You're stunned. The car stops with a halt and you use its bumper to steady yourself. How did that happen?

You check the contents of your bags. Your groceries are smushed; you're going to have to run back in and get new items (or ask the idiot driver of this car to get you new items). You might even have to cancel the dinner at this point. Great; so much for trying to hurry up and get home to start cooking.

The driver of the car starts to get out of the car, slowly. She's a very sweet-looking, clearly very old, woman. She probably just didn't see you.

What do you do?

A. Tell her frankly that she needs to be more careful—or perhaps not drive anymore—and ask that she pay you for the groceries she's ruined.

B. Quickly tell her you're fine and rush away.

C. Make sure the woman is okay, then ask to call someone in her family so you can explain the situation. She probably shouldn't be driving anymore.

D. Help her out of the car and make sure she's okay. The impact of her car may have injured her.

E. Pretty much lose your temper—she could have killed you, or someone else, or even herself with her complete recklessness.

F. Take down her insurance information just in case you're injured (neck injuries often take time to reveal themselves, or so you've read).

QUIZ #9

THE CHEATING BOYFRIEND

You're out to dinner with your family on a Tuesday night at a local restaurant. You notice that many of the booths are empty as you glance around the room to do a little people-watching while you wait for your entrée to arrive. There are a few other families, an old couple, and a guy and a girl about your age, snuggled close together in a cozy corner booth.

Wait a minute. You know that guy. That's your friend's boyfriend, Zach.

Your friend and Zach have only been "official" for five months, but she's super into him and, until this moment, you thought the feeling was mutual. You crane your neck to get a better look. The girl and Zach both have brown hair and brown eyes. Maybe she's his sister (does Zach *have* a sister?) or his cousin. Maybe she's just a friend. You can't jump to conclusions.

You excuse yourself to go to the bathroom so you can sneak a closer look. You don't want him to see you, so you go the long way around the restaurant, using the room's mirrors to get a glance of what's going on at their booth. You can see that, under the table, his hand is on her knee. *Definitely* not something you do to your sister, or cousin, or even a good friend.

Back at your table, you pick at your food, too distracted by Zach and his lady friend. Then you see him kiss her—a sure sign that he's cheating on your pal. The *nerve*.

What do you do?

A. Go right up to Zach, interrupting his "date," and tell him he's a total scumbag.

B. Stay out of it. It's not your business.

C. Call your friend as soon as you get home and break the news in full detail. This isn't something you keep to yourself.

D. Ask the waitress to send a note over to their table, then wave at him when you see he got it. The act is up, buddy.

E. Weigh whether it would hurt your friend more to find out from you now, or to find out on her own after the fact—then proceed down whichever path you think would cause her less pain.

F. Send Zach an e-mail telling him he needs to come clean ASAP. It's not your place to tell her; it's his.

QUIZ #10

THE BOUTIQUE HEIST

You and a friend are shopping in your favorite boutique—it has a ton of affordable, super cute clothing and jewelry. And since the mom of a girl from school owns the place, you guys get a special student discount, which is pretty sweet.

You're focused on finding a great dress for a party this weekend, so you busy yourself with a couple selections and head on into the dressing room. Your friend gravitates between looking at your options and checking out the wares at the accessories station, trying on various necklaces and bracelets. After about a half hour of trying on dresses, you find one you love and your friend approves. Done and done.

While you pay for your dress, your friend again busies herself with trying on necklaces, assessing various pendant shapes and chain lengths, but she doesn't commit to buying anything—she says she wants to think about it first.

You guys leave the store and, a couple minutes later, your friend asks if you notice anything different about her. You study her face, her hair. You check her shoes. Nothing.

She points to the pendant hanging from her neck—it's one of the necklaces she tried on in the store. At first you're confused, wondering when she bought it. While you were in the dressing room?

Then her face breaks out in a sneaky grin as she reveals that she stole it. She just walked right out of the store with it on. She continues going on and on about how it was the biggest thrill of her life—the scariest thing she's ever done, she assures you.

What's your reaction?

A. Grab her hand and drag her back to the store so she can fess up.

B. Shoplifting sounds kind of exciting, to be honest. You ask her to teach you her tricks so you can try it just once.

C. Lie and tell her you think it's no big deal. Not worth fighting about.

D. You don't say much to your friend because you don't want her to know you're disappointed in her. But you go back to the store later in the week and buy some jewelry to go with your dress because you feel bad.

E. Warn your friend that the fine for shoplifting in your town is hundreds of dollars and that it's probably not a good idea to keep doing this—she'll get caught eventually; it's only a matter of probability.

F. Tell her she needs to go back into the store and return the item—or you will.

QUIZ #11

THE HONEST ADVICE

A friend of yours wants to open a restaurant. She's an awesome cook, has worked at a bunch of places as a waitress, and has recently moved up to be an assistant manager, so she feels like the next best step is to break out and start her own place when she's done with school.

She's smart and capable, so she thinks she can handle just about anything. From what you've seen of her work ethic, she's got the chops to start something of her own, but you worry that she might be in over her head. Does she really understand what it takes to own a business?

She comes to you asking for some honest advice: Should she pursue her passion and open a restaurant now? Or should she take the less risky route and go to restaurant management school, make some solid contacts, and maybe pair up with someone in a couple years to start her first place?

What do you tell her?

A. You tell her that you believe in her but that you have some reservations about how it might all play out.

B. Present her two options back to her with possible outcomes and pros and cons so she can weigh them for herself, but you don't tell her what to do.

C. It takes more courage to start a business, in your opinion. It's risky, but you're a risk taker, so you advise her to go for it.

D. You tell her that most restaurants fail and you think it's a bad idea.

E. You think that going to school and learning as much as she can about the industry is the best way to proceed, so that's what you advise.

F. You encourage her to follow her dream (that's what she wants to hear) and offer your help in any capacity to get her started.

QUIZ #12

THE SUSPENSION

You're *so* not a morning person, and it's a struggle for you to get out of bed most mornings. As a result of your sluggishness, you've been late to school these past two weeks more often than not.

Now, we're not talking crazy late, just a couple of minutes here and there. But sometimes you've missed morning roll call, something that your teachers are supposed to be marking down on their rosters. Some of them have obviously been keeping track of you because you've already had to serve a detention for being late three times.

So when you get called into the principal's office one day, you're not really thrown off guard. You figure you'll explain that you've been under a lot of stress lately (and studying a ton!) and that you're super, super sorry for being late.

The principal calls you in and you're all ready to give her your best excuses. However, sitting on her desk, facing you, is a piece of paper with the words "Suspension Notice" written on it in bold, scary letters. She proceeds to tell you that, as per school policy, three tardies is a detention and six is a one-day suspension. You knew that, but you thought that maybe, since you're such a good student, your teachers would just let you slide with one detention and leave it at that. Nope, not so much.

The principal tells you that you need to serve your suspension tomorrow. That means that you have to stay home, and that your parents will totally ask you why you're not getting ready for school. Unless, of course, you pretend to go to school but then go hang out at the mall or somewhere all day, just so they don't find out. (Though that's also risky; if you hang at the mall, you might get in trouble with the police for being truant—they'll think you're ditching.)

Do you tell your parents the truth?

A. No, you don't want to worry them.
B. No, it may cause a fight.
C. No, they don't need to know everything about your life.
D. No, you don't want them to think less of you.
E. Yes, even though you don't want to.
F. Of course. You tell your parents everything.

QUIZ #13

THE JEANS

Your sister is about to go on her first date after suffering through a rough breakup with her (now ex) boyfriend four months ago. She met a guy at work and she's actually really excited to go out with him—a big change from rejecting any guy who asked her out over the past few months. In fact, you think she's looking forward to this first date more than she did her first date with her ex.

You're sitting on her bed while she shows you what she plans to wear on the date. She wants your opinion on which shoes she should pair with her outfit, because she's having a fashion crisis. She puts on a top and wiggles into her jeans before sliding on the first pair of heels in contention. But you can't focus on the shoes—it's her jeans that are the problem.

The wash is too light for her figure and the jeans look about a size too small. Which is crazy because your sister is in great shape and looks good in basically everything she wears. There's just something not right about these jeans. You're not sure why she even bought them. She should not wear them on this date . . . or ever.

You ask her to try on the second pair of shoes while you figure out how (or if) to tell her that she needs to rethink the entire outfit for the sake of her love life. You want her to look her best and feel confident on this date.

What do you tell her?

A. You suggest your favorite dress from your own closet for her to wear instead—you know she's been eyeing it and it will look fantastic on her. Plus, it goes better with her favorite heels, you convince her.

B. You ask her what she likes about the jeans, hoping to lead her to conclude that they are not well suited to her.

C. You try to be noncommittal about your feelings on the jeans but drop hints that they might not be the best choice. You don't want to offend her.

D. You reason that your sister is more likely to get a second date with the guy if she looks her best, yet wonder if she wants to be with a guy who's focused on looks. Although since first impressions are so important, you advise her to find something else to wear.

E. You tell her the jeans are not flattering and that she should donate them.

F. You say the jeans are too tame for a first date and rifle through her closet to find something sexier for her to wear.

QUIZ #14

THE LYING EYES

One day at lunch, your so-called rival at school starts telling a long-winded story about her spring break. She has a crowd of other students around her at the table next to yours, rapt in awe.

She tells the group that her parents took her to Paris over the vacation and starts talking about all the amazing restaurants they went to, how great the view is from the top of the Eiffel Tower, and what kinds of stores she shopped in. She says her mom even bought her a handmade silk dress that she's going to wear to the spring formal next month and a designer purse that was so expensive, she's not allowed to bring it to school.

Everyone is hanging on to her every word at this point, and she knows it. She looks over at your table to check if you and your friends are listening in—and she looks smug seeing that you are. Even your pals are oohing and ahhing over the details.

The funny thing is, you're pretty sure that she didn't go anywhere over the break. In fact, unbeknownst to her, you spotted her at the mall, right smack in the middle of vacation, shopping with her mom and her little brother. So, clearly, she wasn't in Paris then.

This is a perfect time for you to completely call out this girl. You know she'd one hundred percent do the same to you if the situation was reversed.

What do you do?

A. First, you check her body language to see if she's telling any shred of truth. (Maybe they went to Paris over a long weekend?) If the signs are there that she's lying, you straight up ask her why she's misleading everyone.

B. You don't want to be confrontational or let her know that you know she's lying, so you just nod and accept what she's saying until you can excuse yourself from the lunch table without anyone noticing.

C. You ask her how the mall in Paris was. Maybe she'll get the hint that you know she's lying.

D. Her lying makes you feel empathetic toward her—surely there's a reason she's not telling the truth and trying to make her spring break sound better than it really was. You smile and try to make her feel comfortable.

E. You get the sense you're being lied to and you don't like it one bit. You cut her off mid-sentence and ask her to tell everyone the name of that "amazing" restaurant she went to so you can look it up on your phone.

F. You know that calling her out in the lie will probably make her want to retaliate against you, so you ask her a lot of questions about her trip, which she struggles to answer. This way, she knows that you know she's lying—but that you're not going to call her out.

QUIZ #15

THE TEST

You have your history midterm coming up and you're already worried that you're not going to do well on it. You practically failed the last quiz you took, even though you studied for days.

A friend of yours tells you that he secured a copy of the test. The teacher left it on the Xerox machine when she was making duplicates, and somehow he got his hands on it. If you want, he will make you a copy and you can use it to fully prepare for the test. No one else knows he has the test and he's not going to tell anyone—this is a guaranteed, foolproof way to ace the test without any risk involved.

You ask to look at the test really quickly and, sure enough, it looks legitimate. The questions appear to be exactly the kinds of questions your teacher would ask, and the date listed on the test is indeed the date the test will be given on—you know your friend has the real, exact copy.

If you use this test to study, you'll get an A+, no problem. Your friend is trying to do you a favor since he knows how poorly you did on the last quiz, and you appreciate that he's looking out for you. Do you want to cheat on a test, though, in order to get a better grade in the class?

What do you do?

A. Tell your friend that, while you appreciate the gesture, this counts as cheating and you're going to tell the teacher that you got a copy of the test so that she can write a new one. It's the right thing to do.

B. Cheating on a test won't actually make you more intelligent—you tell your friend no thanks; you're going to study extra hard instead of using the test copy.

C. While you don't like the idea of cheating, the idea of doing something dangerous sounds exciting to you. Plus, you'll get a better grade. You decide to get a copy of the test and take your chances.

D. You tell your friend thank you and take a copy, but you don't use it. You don't want your friend to be put off, since he was trying to help you, but it's not worth risking getting in trouble or making the teacher mad.

E. You say thanks but no thanks, but you don't tell the teacher.

F. You take a copy of the test to please your friend (he was looking out for you, after all) and then write an anonymous note to the teacher telling her that a copy of the test is floating around. That way, your friend doesn't get in trouble and your teacher isn't deceived.

QUIZ #16

THE JOB INTERVIEW

You're in the middle of an interview for your dream job. The head of the company is asking you questions about your background, your strengths, and your career path. You're answering each one easily and, from the look on her face, you think your answers must impress her (the CEO!). She's nodding along with your responses and appears to really like you, based on her tone of voice and her gestures.

Then she utters the question that is notoriously asked on every job interview: What do you see as your biggest weakness in the workplace? The question feels like a trap. Answer honestly and she may decide that, despite liking all of your responses so far, you're not a good fit for the team.

This is one of those "damned if you do, damned if you don't" situations that feels like you'll be wrong no matter which path you choose. You try to stall and get a better sense of what she's looking for by asking if she means technical skills or personality weaknesses. But you know that, no matter what she says, you're still going to have to come up with an answer that doesn't make you look bad, yet also satisfies her that you're actually addressing her question.

What do you do?

A. You share some negative feedback you received from your previous boss and explain how you worked on this issue.

B. Admit that you're a little thrown off by the question, but tell her you want to give her your most honest answer. May as well get it all out there so there are no surprises if she hires you.

C. You decide to be up front about a couple of your weaknesses, but a little guarded. You're not sure you completely trust her intentions.

D. Tell her what you think is your most flattering "flaw" (that you tend to overwork yourself) and hope it suffices.

E. Give a passive response about how certain people see some characteristics as flaws, yet others see them as positives—since you aren't sure which flaws she herself possesses, you don't want to offend her.

F. You give her a list of your many shortcomings and how you discovered them. You want to make sure you're giving her what she's looking for.

QUIZ #17

THE WRONG NAME

It's your first day at a brand-new school and your homeroom teacher is going down the class roster, name by name. Each student is supposed to stand up and say a couple words about him or herself—a nickname you may have, your favorite sport, what you did over the summer break. The point is to give a few details to the class (and to your teacher) so that everyone can get to know each other, at least a little bit.

Since you're a new student, this introduction is everyone's very first impression of you. You'll be defined by this moment, in many ways. So you want to make a good impression, yet stay true to who you are.

You're pretty far down on the list, so you have a chance to listen to what the other students say before it's your turn. Some people give alternate names (Steven wants to be called Stevie, for example) and some talk about their pets and where they went on vacation.

Then it's your turn. You've planned out what you're going to say already, but when the teacher says your name he completely butchers it, totally throwing you off. You have to decide if you're going to correct him or not, and how.

What do you do?

A. Use this as an opportunity to reinvent yourself. You give yourself a nickname instead of your given name (which you never liked anyway) and tell the class that's what you prefer to be called.

B. You don't correct him. You don't want to be bothersome or disruptive.

C. You don't correct him in the moment—you worry that might embarrass your teacher. So you say your spiel and then hand the teacher a note at the end of class with the correct pronunciation.

D. You correct your teacher right away—there's no reason not to be honest about how to say your name.

E. You correct your teacher in the moment, quickly.

F. You correct your teacher immediately and give him the full etymology of where your name comes from and what it means.

QUIZ #18

THE WEDDING

You're getting married in six months and you're right in the thick of wedding planning. You've chosen the venue, the vendors, and (of course) the groom, but now it's time to make all of those little decisions about the food, the decor, and the ambiance.

Your husband-to-be is pretty much down for anything (as many grooms are) but your respective sets of parents have some big ideas on what kind of wedding you two should have. They want everything to be beautiful and lavish, which is not really your thing. In fact, if you and your fiancé could host a backyard barbecue with some great music and dancing, that would be perfect.

Your parents, however, believe that you should serve a plated, three-course meal with numerous options for people with food allergies and people who are vegetarian. Your future in-laws want sparkling china and glassware, and personalized place cards to make the event look luxe. And because your parents and in-laws are footing the bill, you feel obligated to take their opinions into account.

Sometimes you feel like this isn't even your wedding, that you're merely a detail in this big-scale production, and that the event is becoming less and less about marriage and more about details that shouldn't matter . . . well, to anyone.

You're going to have to make some decisions about these details in the next week or so, and the clock is ticking.

How do you proceed with your wedding planning?

A. You say screw the whole thing and decide to elope instead.

B. You pick your battles. It's not worth the time and effort to try to control everything, so you focus only on the details that really matter to you and explain why you want those things to be your way.

C. You and your partner sit down with your parents and your future in-laws to come clean about not being happy with the direction things are going in, and request that changes be made.

D. The wedding isn't about you—it's about your family. So you cheerfully help your parents and your in-laws with their ideas for the wedding.

E. You're just ready for the planning to be over and you don't want any drama, so you keep quiet about your feelings.

F. You and your partner reason that spending so much money on one day is a terrible financial investment. You ask your parents to put the funds toward your college loans or future home instead, if they really want to spend it.

QUIZ #19

THE LOVE TRIANGLE

It's homecoming season, and all anyone can talk about is who is going to ask who when. Text messages are buzzing around campus bearing alerts and rumors about which girls may be asked next.

Your best friend suddenly gets a text saying that this super nice guy named Jeff from your Spanish class is probably going to ask you tomorrow. Which is super weird because you and Jeff's best friend, Dave, flirt all the time in Geometry, and Dave's hinted more than once that he plans on asking you.

You're not sure if Dave knows that Jeff is planning on asking you, and vice versa. So you ask your BFF to text her source back to find out more. Apparently, Jeff has had his eye on you for a long time and just told Dave, and even though Dave really likes you, he doesn't want to hurt Jeff by asking you to the dance. But he's still contemplating if he's going to do it or not. He liked you before Jeff did, but he never actually told Jeff, so he doesn't want to cause a weird situation between them. Which is frustrating, because you actually like Dave, and Jeff will only be a friend to you.

Ugh. Drama. What do you do?

A. Hide whenever you see one of them around campus and never let yourself be alone with either of them until after homecoming. Maybe that way, neither of them will ask you and the whole thing will blow over.

B. Have your friend tell the source that you like Dave and would rather go with him—you have to be true to yourself.

C. Just be patient and go with whichever guy asks you first. That's the fairest thing to do.

D. Go find Dave and ask him to prom—why beat around the bush?

E. Reason that there is no possible positive outcome of this situation, because someone is bound to get hurt and a friendship is at stake. You go with one of your guy friends instead.

F. Decide that you'll say no to both of them so you don't have to choose.

QUIZ #20

THE UNWANTED ADVANCE

You're at your local pizzeria with your friends after soccer practice, noshing on some slices. It's been a long day and you're so glad you can just unwind and relax with your girls.

You see an obnoxious group of guys standing a couple feet away, huddled around one of those old video game machines. They keep looking over at you and your pals and whispering. You really, really hope they leave you alone. You are not in the mood to have to deal with random guys trying to chat you up. You ignore them and focus on your conversation with your friends.

Then the chair next to you opens up and, sure enough, one the guys sidles over and plops down beside you. He nudges you and tries to strike up a conversation, but the last thing you want to do right now is make small talk with some random guy. Sure, he's probably nice enough, but you're in no mood to get hit on. (Especially because you'll miss all the gossip your girls are probably divulging right now.)

But he's sitting next to you, asking you questions, totally unaware that you don't want to talk to him.

What do you do?

A. Tell him straightforwardly that you are not interested and you'd like to get back to your friends.

B. Feign interest in the conversation to not hurt his feelings or cause any conflict.

C. Talk with him and engage in conversation until he asks you out on a date—which you accept because you know it will make him happy.

D. Tell him that he seems like a super nice guy and direct him toward another cute girl across the restaurant.

E. Do a quick cost/benefit analysis on the guy to see if he could actually be someone you want to date: Does he seem like your type? Does he look like he showers regularly? Does he have a nice smile?

F. Scare him off by telling him something that will make him wary of you—like how your last boyfriend didn't date anyone for a year after you broke his heart.

QUIZ #21

THE EXCHANGE STUDENT

You're plugging away at your homework when, all of a sudden, your allergies start really acting up. Your nose and eyes are running, you feel the urge to sneeze—you're not sure what's going on. You reach for a tissue and wonder if you're getting sick.

You check your desk: There's no dust, no clutter, no reason for you to be having this reaction. You're pretty sensitive to things, so you try to keep your area neat and tidy, free of anything that might set you off.

You remember that, this very morning, the exchange student your family is hosting was showing off the new, expensive designer candle that she got from her boyfriend back home as a birthday gift. She was so excited about the candle because it combines her favorite scents and was the first big present he's ever bought her. You sniff the air and, as you get a bigger whiff of a tuberose and peony fragrance, you full-on sneeze louder than you ever have before.

Clearly, this candle is doing something to your senses, and it's not good. You really want to ask your new housemate to snuff it, box it, and get rid of it so you can get on with your day. But is that something you can ask of her? What are the boundaries with personal space (and personal scents) when living in close quarters?

What do you do?

A. Go to her room and blow out the candle, then tell her she can't light it up again because you're allergic.
B. Tell her you're having a bad reaction to the candle and that you'd really appreciate it if she wouldn't burn it while you're at home.
C. Buy a desk fan just in case she lights it again.
D. Say nothing but blow your nose loudly and hope that she gets the message. If not, oh well.
E. Suffer in silence. She seemed really stoked about her new candle.
F. Check the internet for evidence of candle-related allergic reactions so you can show her when you ask her to stop using it—it's better to have clear proof in these situations.

QUIZ #22

THE BASKETBALL TEAM

You're the varsity basketball team's star player and try-outs have just ended. The coach calls you into his office to go over the final list of who's making the team and who's being cut—he wants your opinion on a couple of the last players that should be added to the roster.

You talk about each person individually, sharing her merits and weaknesses from your perspective with your coach until you get down to the two final potential players. It comes down to your best friend and a new girl who could become the star of the team.

Your best friend is a great team player who excels at passing and keeping morale high. But she just barely made varsity last year, and her skills have not improved over the season's break. She worked out and trained a bit, but basketball was never as important to her as it is to you. Still, everyone knows and loves her. She gets everyone pumped up and excited to get out onto the court before a game.

The new girl is an all-star in the making. She's strong, her skills are sharp, and you know that she could help your team make it all the way to the state championships. But, she's quiet and keeps to herself. This could be because she's new at school and doesn't quite feel like she fits in yet. Or she might not be the best teammate. Only time will tell.

But time is the one thing you don't have. The coach wants you to choose between your BFF and this new girl for the final spot on the team right now.

Who do you choose?

A. You choose your BFF but tell the coach that, next time, you really don't want to be put in this awkward position.

B. You tell the coach that both players can take your spot on the team. You don't want to choose.

C. You choose the better player and you tell your BFF about the decision you made before the cut list goes up. That's the honest thing to do.

D. You choose your BFF. The other girl won't feel badly about being cut, but your friend will.

E. You choose the better player—you want the fiercest, best team possible so you can dominate the league.

F. You choose the better player—if your team does well, there's a higher chance that you might get a scholarship.

QUIZ #23

THE CHEER-UP

It's Wednesday afternoon and you just got home. On your way to the living room to watch TV, you hear your brother crying (and trying to be quiet about it) in his room. This is very uncharacteristic of him. He hardly ever gets emotional, let alone cries. You knock softly on his door and push it open a little. He's sitting on the floor, his eyes red-rimmed. He doesn't like anyone seeing him get upset and rolls his eyes when he sees you, but tells you to come on in anyway.

He's had the worst day ever: He failed his math test, and he found out that he didn't make the cut for the school debate team. Even worse, he finally worked up the courage to go talk to the girl he's been crushing on for a whole year, only to find out that she now has a boyfriend. Every area of his life totally sucks right now, he says.

Basically, he's hurt, he's pissed, and he's mad at himself. (Not to mention, he's pretty worried about how his math test is going to affect his overall grade.) Plus, there are still two more days left in the school week to go until the weekend. He really needs some cheering up—and fast.

How do you help him feel better?

A. Give him a big hug and suggest taking him out for comfort food.

B. Listen patiently and calmly to him, and tell him that he can talk about everything for as long as he'd like.

C. Tell him to buck up and take him to a boxing class so he can let off some steam.

D. Offer to tutor him in math for the rest of the semester to help him boost his grade.

E. Comfort him, then ask if he wants to watch TV with you in the living room.

F. Be frank: Nothing you can do or say right now is going to solve anything or change what happened, but you'll try to help him feel better as soon as possible.

QUIZ #24

THE GROUP PROJECT

You're taking a business class and, for the midterm, the teacher asks you to break up into teams of five to complete a group project. Your task is to come up with an idea for any kind of local business you think would thrive in your town, and then to write a business plan as well as pitch the idea to the class and your teacher. You have two weeks to complete this project.

The project counts for one-third of your entire class grade. And your group will be graded as a whole—there are no individual grades based on how much work each person did.

You find four other people to work with you and start talking about your ideas. So far, everyone seems enthusiastic and excited to create something awesome together. However, as the discussion goes on, you can start to see personalities emerge: who is going to actually do the work, who is just going to coast through, who has really good ideas, and who just likes to hear him- or herself talk. This is going to be a long couple of weeks.

Finally, by the end of the class period, you collectively settle on an idea. Now it's time to divide up the work and actually complete the project components themselves.

What is your role in the group?

A. You end up doing the bulk of the work. That's typically what happens in these group project situations.

B. You tell the group that you can only commit to doing two specific pieces of this project (you have three other tests coming up) and you follow through on your word.

C. You sit back and watch the group figure it all out. You'll do whatever job is left, if there is one.

D. You volunteer to handle the presentation to the class—you don't mind speaking in front of people.

E. You hate the idea of your grade being dependent on other people's work, so you ask to do the final proofreading for the written component—then end up changing most of the work everyone else did so it's up to your standards.

F. You start doing the bulk of the work, then send out an e-mail to the more responsible people in the group asking them for help.

QUIZ #25

THE RUSH DECISION

It's your first week of college, and all of the campus clubs have set up booths in the main quad so freshmen can learn more about the ones they might want to join.

You and your new roommate head over there to check it out. You're excited to make new friends and be a part of clubs that you really care about—not just join the ones that boost your profile on a college application.

Soon enough, you come across the sorority and fraternity booths and you start perusing your options. There are surprisingly a lot of different houses, each with its own vibe or focus. There's really something for everyone.

You know that Greek life is pretty big at your school, so you decide to join your roommate in signing up for rush. The process lasts two weeks and, at each event, you learn more about the houses, what they're all about, and how you might fit in. You meet a ton of really interesting people—and a ton of really *not* interesting people—in the process. All of this allows you to start to determine which house feels like it would be the best one for you.

Finally, it's the last day of rush, and you need to make your decision of what house you'll officially call your own.

Which one do you choose?

A. You choose the coed business fraternity. It will be awesome for networking purposes.

B. You didn't feel like you fit into any house, so you decide to drop out of the process without choosing one.

C. You choose the house with the notoriously intense initiation process. Go big or go home, right?

D. You choose the house your roommate wants to be in; that way you guys won't be rivals.

E. You choose the house that's most focused on philanthropy. Being part of the Greek system is a great way to give back.

F. You choose the house with the members that seem most authentic to you. You wouldn't change who you are just to join a social club. And if it turns out that people in the house are fake, you'll drop out.

QUIZ #26

THE FAMILY SECRET

You're in the attic in your parents' house, looking for your old homecoming dresses. There's so much stuff up here—boxes and boxes and boxes. You could spend hours going through family artifacts and photos. But you try to stay on task. You promised your friend's little sister that she could borrow one of your dresses for her Halloween costume, and you need to try to find them today.

As you weave around piles of papers and endless stuff, you see a small wooden box nailed shut. The top of the box reads "For my family" written in a thick black marker. You've never seen this box in your life, and you're not sure if others have either—it looks like it's never been opened.

You find a hammer among your dad's old tools and start prying open the box. After pulling out seven rusted nails, you can finally wrench the lid off. Inside, there are a bunch of papers, all covered in a thin layer of dust. On top is a letter. You look at who signed it—it's your grandfather's name. He passed away ten years ago.

As you start to read, you realize that the letter is a confession. Your grandfather says he was involved in a money-laundering scheme years ago, unknown to anyone in the family. He nearly lost every penny he had. To keep himself afloat, he went to the police and told on the others within the group, with whom we was laundering money, and the police paid him handsomely for his insider information. His partners in crime went to jail while he remained free and went about his life largely unscathed.

The information shocks you and is quite disturbing. Your grandfather was a sweet, mild-mannered man—and now it turns out that he was really a criminal? And that he turned on his unlawful friends?

What do you do with this information?

A. You show your family right away, of course. To not do so would feel like a lie.

B. While you know that what you discovered will shock your family, you don't believe in withholding information from people, so you show them what you found.

C. You put yourself in your family's shoes. Would they want to know the truth? If so, you show them.

D. You sit on the information for a couple weeks, then talk to a friend to see if you should tell your parents what you found.

E. Your instinct is to destroy the time capsule. You thought your grandfather was a brave, honorable man, and now everything you thought you knew has been questioned.

F. You don't want to upset anyone, so you leave the time capsule up there for someone else to find eventually.

QUIZ #27

THE ILLNESS

You've been having some really serious headaches lately so you decide to go to the doctor to check things out. After doing some blood tests, your doctor orders you to have an MRI to have a better look inside your body.

You go through the scanner, and the doctor says something is wrong. There is a large mass in your brain and it needs to be biopsied. You let the surgeon go in and check out what's going on inside your head, fearing the worst.

After your procedure, the doctor informs you that the surgeon was able to remove the mass and that your headaches will likely be gone from now on. However, he also has some very bad news: You have brain cancer.

A couple more rounds of tests give you your prognosis. You have a year to live. There's no cure for the rare type of cancer you have, and the doctor doesn't know how you got it. These things just happen sometimes; a terrible chance illness struck you for reasons unknown.

Because you only have a year, you could decide not to work or go to school any longer. You could spend this last year any way you choose. There's no reason not to.

How do you spend your final year?

A. Reading and learning as much as you can, so you can invent something awesome before your time is up.

B. Conquering every crazy item on your bucket list.

C. Honestly? You'd try to get on the Make-A-Wish Foundation list and see if you could take advantage of any positive experiences that come with having a terminal illness.

D. Devoting yourself to others with your illness, volunteering, and making yourself as useful as you can.

E. Being true to yourself and living life as you normally would sounds best to you, if only because it makes you feel more normal.

F. Spending time relaxing and being with family and friends.

QUIZ #28

THE TERM PAPER

It's your last class of the day and you're already looking out the window, daydreaming of what you're going to do once the bell rings. Rush home to read the book you're currently engrossed in? Grab a snack with your friends? The possibilities seem endless. Anywhere sounds better than being here right now. It's been a long week. Thank goodness tomorrow is Friday.

Your teacher just made some kind of announcement about a term paper, so you snap back to attention. She repeats herself for good measure, reminding the class, yet again, that your twenty-page final term paper is due tomorrow.

What?!

You flip through your school planner to tomorrow's date. You don't have any record of a paper being due tomorrow. You turn the page to the next week. Nothing. Then the next. And right there, on Friday two weeks from now you see it: Term Paper Due.

You somehow wrote down the paper information on the wrong date by accident. This paper is basically your class final—there isn't a written test given at the end of the semester. If you don't do well on the paper, you may get a way lower grade in the class overall. Plus, you were hoping to ask your teacher for a recommendation for your college application. If you don't turn in the assignment—and do a good job—will she still vouch for you? Probably not...

What do you do?

A. Do the best you can to finish on time, then ask a friend to proofread the paper.

B. Talk to the teacher after class and admit that you wrote down the wrong date. Ask if she would grant you a two-day extension so you could have the weekend to work on the paper.

C. Work tirelessly all night until the paper's finished—you wouldn't dream of turning something in late and jeopardizing your grade.

D. Take a chance and turn the assignment in on Monday, so you have more time to work on it. Maybe the teacher won't notice.

E. Work on the assignment until it's done, turn it in, and hope for the best.

F. It's no one's fault but your own that you got the date wrong. You do the best you can on the paper, turn it in when it's due, and include a note to the teacher apologizing for your rushed work.

QUIZ #29

THE TIME MACHINE

The United States government has announced that they have built a working time machine and they are looking for one individual to go into the future to see what the world is like in a century's time.

Anyone who is interested in being considered should fill out the online application detailing why they are the best person for the job. Because you're a curious person, you put your name in for consideration. Why not you, right?

Somehow, some way, the government chooses you to go to the future and to be the country's representative of the past. You are prepared for your journey with a special suit (in case the elements have changed), and a GoPro to record what you see and hear. You'll only be gone for one hour to check out what lies ahead, and then you will be beamed back into the present to give your report. Your task is to talk to as many people as possible in those sixty minutes to learn what you can about life in the future.

You get prepared to go and you are transported to the future. The air is still breathable and people look like us, except their heads are much, much larger. Every person seems to be wearing a contraption on their heads that doubles as a phone and computer. Most systems are automated; for example, there are no bus drivers, only self-driving buses. You start finding people to talk to, and record your interviews.

You finish your mission and it's time to go home. When the government watches your video, what do they see in your conversations and interactions with people?

A. You focused mainly on asking people about advances and innovations—how life had changed from a technological standpoint.

B. You talked to people about how they were feeling about their lives and what their view of their current time period was.

C. You asked people for an honest assessment of the past—how they viewed us from their perspective, and what criticisms they had.

D. You wanted to know about national security measures and which countries were currently at war.

E. You inquired about the rates of homelessness and unemployment, wanting to understand the gap between rich and poor in the future, and what can be done now to fix it.

F. You asked people to describe their world in one sentence so you could see if common themes within their responses emerged.

QUIZ #30

THE ISLAND

You wake up one morning lying on a beach. You blink your eyes and rub them hard, totally confused. All you hear are crashing waves, rustling trees, and a bird or two calling in the distance. Where in the world are you?

You stand up and take account of your surroundings. There's a sandy beach littered with driftwood and an endless sea in front of you. Behind you, all you see are thick trees, some kind of jungle. You're wearing a T-shirt and shorts, with your old tennis shoes laced on your feet. The air is warm and balmy.

You have no idea how you got here and no idea how you will get home. All you know is that the sun is directly overhead, meaning it must be close to noon, and you may in fact be in this place for a long, long time.

You shout down the beach, calling out "Hello!" There's no answer, only more rustling of tree branches. You walk twenty paces toward the jungle and almost trip over a navy canvas bag that looks brand-new. Your heart beats faster, hoping that this bag contains something useful that will help you survive in this unknown paradise.

Ideally, what would this bag contain?

A. A knife to fend off attackers, if necessary, and to hunt for food.

B. A cell phone, so you could call your parents and let them know you're okay.

C. Food; you could use it for sustenance and possibly trade it with locals, if there are any.

D. A selection of gifts that you could use as an offering to make friends with the island's inhabitants.

E. A guidebook on how to survive in the wild so you can, well, survive.

F. A note explaining how the heck you got to the island, and how to get home.

QUIZ #31

THE DEVICE

You're a seasoned reporter who writes articles for a leading technology website. Today, the world's largest global telecommunications company is unveiling a brand-new product—something that will change the way we connect with people as we know it. It's more significant than the iPhone and possibly more life changing than even the Internet. It's not another computer or a cell phone or a tablet—it's something far more advanced. This new product will help us connect to family and friends through space and time, transport us around the world in a matter of seconds, and even allow us to see our futures. It's very advanced technology, beyond our wildest dreams. It's something we never conceived could be possible. Everyone is waiting to see and hear what bloggers have only been able to speculate about for months.

You have an exclusive interview with the woman who invented the device, and you get to be the very first person to pick her brain about this new technology, how she devised it, and what her intentions are for its use. Your job is to ask the questions your readers want the answers to, so the world at large can better understand—and embrace—this technological achievement.

What's your first question to the inventor?

A. How does it work?
B. How will it change our daily lives?
C. Can I try it out?
D. How will it be used for the greater good?
E. How does it help us?
F. Why do we need it?

QUIZ #32

THE
EQUATION

It's been a long afternoon of homework and your brain is basically mush. You left your math problems until last, and now you're plowing through them on autopilot in an effort to finish before your favorite TV show is on.

You get to the last problem and you're stumped. No matter how many times you work it out or how carefully you compute the numbers, your answer just doesn't add up. You look online to refresh yourself with the concepts and re-read the textbook section about these types of equations, your eyes tracking each word very carefully as to not miss a single ounce of information. You even pull out your class notes to make sure there aren't any pieces of knowledge missing.

Okay. You sharpen your pencil and work the problem out on a fresh piece of paper. This time, it has to work. Each step, you take extra care and pay extra attention to the task at hand. Finally, you're calculating the end result . . . and yet again, it just doesn't add up.

You're starting to get frustrated. Your show starts in an hour and there is no end in sight with this equation. You have no idea what you are overlooking here.

What do you do next?

A. Keep working at it until it's solved, even if you miss your show and it takes you all night. You would never turn your homework in unfinished.

B. Send a group e-mail out to the class to check on everyone else; they must all be just as frustrated.

C. Phone the textbook company to make sure there isn't an error or typo.

D. Call a friend and see if he is having the same issue; maybe you can help each other?

E. Leave it unsolved—you can ask the teacher for guidance tomorrow.

F. Get your frustration out by going for a long run, then come back to the problem later after watching your show.

QUIZ #33

THE UNEXPECTED BIRTHDAY REQUEST

Your friend's birthday is coming up, so one afternoon you ask her what she's planning on doing. These days, people don't usually have formal birthday parties. They're more likely to ask everyone to come to dinner or go out somewhere in town. Something fun and special, but also an activity you might do on any typical Friday night.

Your friend says she's actually been toying around with an out-of-the-box birthday idea and she would love your opinion on it. She wants to get the whole group together to do something that will allow her to check off an item on her bucket list: bungee jumping.

Your stomach plunges to the ground. The idea of bungee jumping sounds terrifying to you. You're scared to death of heights, and the last thing you would ever sign up for is to plunge off of a bridge or ravine or what have you with an elastic cord strapped to your feet.

Your friend keeps chatting away, not seeing your discomfort. She knows bungee jumping isn't for everyone, but it's her birthday and people should be excited to have an excuse to do something daring, right? Then you hear your friend ask you, "What do you think about my idea?"

What do you tell her?

A. You tell your friend you'll have to think about it.

B. Yes, heights scare the pants off you, but you actually like doing things that terrify you, so you say yes on the spot.

C. You have some serious trepidation, and say you're going to research the physics behind bungee jumping and the probability of risk involved before saying yes or no.

D. You're scared, but you know this will mean a lot to your friend, so you tell her it's an awesome idea and you agree to go.

E. You tell your friend that you love her, but you're not willing to do something that terrifies you (or could kill you).

F. Not wanting to tell her no, you say you'll do it. But the day of the jump, you'll tell your friend that you're sick. That way, she won't be mad at you.

QUIZ #34

THE DUEL

You've been transported back to the Wild West and, by some odd twist of fate, you're the new cowboy in town. You're at the saloon chatting with the local folks and trying to understand this new world you've been thrown into.

There's a very pretty woman who keeps peeking into the saloon window, and you can't help but notice her. You excuse yourself from your conversation and go outside to introduce yourself. Her name is Anna, and she's very pleased to make your acquaintance. She says she has to get back home and hustles away. You turn back to the saloon to plant yourself on your barstool again.

Just then, you feel a hand on your shoulder. It belongs to a gruff-looking, grizzled man who's at least a head taller than you. He wants to know why you were flirting with his fiancée.

Oops.

You assure him that you were simply introducing yourself, but he's raging mad. He won't tolerate you trying to steal his woman, he says, talking about Anna as if she were his property. The situation escalates and he tells you that it's either you or him in this town. He's challenging you to a duel.

In two weeks' time, he says, you'll meet him in the town square with your best pistol. If you don't show up, you're not only banished from town but you're a rotten coward at that.

You know that there's no defending yourself verbally against this man. He seems to think that you've engaged in an illicit affair with his bride-to-be, and he's not hearing reason. All you did was talk to her, after all. It looks like a duel, death, or banishment (or a combination thereof) are your only options.

What do you do?

A. Accept the duel and determine that you'll have to allow yourself to get shot first. You don't want to kill anyone.

B. Say that you do not accept his challenge and that you're a coward to get out of it. You leave town immediately.

C. Accept the terms of the duel and train for the next two weeks to prepare yourself so that you can win—you're not afraid of death, but you want the glory.

D. Accept and hope you win—the world will be a better place with one less jerk.

E. Tell him that duels are ridiculous and that you'd rather challenge him to a mind game.

F. Since fifty-fifty odds sound risky, you choose to leave town rather than take your chances. Your life is too valuable.

QUIZ #35

THE DARK ALLEY

You're walking home from a party with some friends around midnight. You're in the neighboring town, but you only have a thirty-minute trip on foot and it's a nice, clear night. While you don't know this area that well, it seems nice enough to be safe—at least on the major streets.

After a couple of blocks, you come to a fork in the road and stop to assess which way you should all go. One path is a well-lit, semi-busy street with a couple of cafés and shops. The other path is a dark alley bearing nothing but a few dumpsters and shallow pools of stagnant water from the recent rain.

According to Google Maps, the alley is the shorter path to your house. It will take you just another five minutes to get home. Taking the street would mean you wouldn't get home for another twenty minutes.

Your friends live on the opposite side of town than you do—in order to get home quicker, they should take the well-lit street.

You're hungry and starting to get a little chilly, so you want to get home as soon as possible. But if you take the short route, you're risking walking down a dark alley for five long minutes all alone.

What do you do?

A. You stick with your friends—you're safer as a group.

B. You take the darker yet shorter alley alone—you're not scared.

C. While it's logical to take the shorter path home in order to get there quicker, it's illogical to take the more dangerous alley path to save fifteen minutes. You take the well-lit street.

D. You don't mind the extra time it will take to get home, so you take the longer street.

E. You admit that the dark alley scares you and walk with your friends.

F. You start down the dark alley, then realize it was a bad idea and run to catch up with your friends.

QUIZ #36

THE BULLY

Ever since you started a new school, you've been having issues with an older girl harassing you. At first, it started with some mild teasing. Then she started following you home. Now she's threatening to beat you up unless you give her whatever allowance money you have on you.

This kid is a little bigger than you, but not by much. With a little training, you could probably take her. But is that the route you want to go? You're not sure you have a choice at this point.

You've tried ignoring her and that doesn't work—she just gets right in your face so you can't ignore her, or blocks your path so you can't escape until you acknowledge her. You tried changing your route home to confuse her—she caught on. You once told her you didn't have any money (you didn't that day) and she shoved you to the ground.

You don't want to tell your parents because if they call the school and the bully's parents, you worry things will just be worse for you, and you really don't want to have to change schools yet again after just transferring.

What's your game plan to stop this bully?

A. Invite the bully to come home with you and play video games.

B. Ask a friend to walk home with you; the bully is less likely to bother you if someone else is around.

C. Give the bully what she wants and accept that this is now part of your life.

D. Outsmart the bully by laughing hysterically at everything she says. Experts say, according to your research, that this can throw the bully off and make her feel powerless.

E. Start practicing martial arts and working out. One day soon, you'll challenge her to a fight in front of everyone at school. When you win, that should shut her up.

F. Develop your inner strength until you feel confident—if you're authentically self-assured, the bully won't feel like she can reign over you.

QUIZ #37

THE WEAPON

You've signed up for a special task force, training with the military so you can apply to join an elite group of soldiers who not only defend the country but help people who are struggling to survive in dire conditions around the world. For months, you've been training your body and mind to be as strong as possible so you might earn a spot in this group.

Today is the last day of your training, and your weeks and weeks of preparation culminate in a test. The general who has overseen your training informs you and the other recruits that you will be dropped into an unknown (to you) territory that may or may not be inhabited. It may or may not be in the midst of war. It may or may not be safe to enter.

That's all he knows—or all he will tell you—and since there aren't any clear details, this information pretty much means nothing. And that's the point. If you join this task force, you'll need to ship off to areas of the world that most people pay little attention to, and who knows what state they will be in when you get there?

Your task is to survive twenty-four hours in the place where you are dropped. To help you, you may choose one survival item from the following selection: a cowbell, a map of the terrain, a gun, night vision goggles, or food for one day.

Which do you choose?

A. The cowbell, so you can alert others around you of danger if necessary.

B. The map, so you know where you are and how to find cover.

C. The gun, so you can defend yourself and others as needed.

D. The night vision goggles, so you can see clearly at all times.

E. The gun, so you can shoot your own food and have some self-defense.

F. The food, so you have sustenance and comfort.

QUIZ #38

THE GYM RATS

You're at the gym one day, just doing your thing. Some biceps, some triceps, a little chest work. It feels good to be lifting weights and getting stronger with each rep, each strain of your muscles. You can almost feel your arms expand with each curl.

You hear laughter and the sound of large weights bouncing on the gym's rubberized floor. A group of guys wearing tank tops is working out next to you, and they're a bit rowdy. Their muscles are quite large and very defined. They could be professional athletes, given their physiques. (Or maybe they just come here *way* too often.) They're grabbing the biggest weights in the room, seeing how much they can bench and how high they can lift. They're a bunch of showoffs, really.

However, their skills are pretty impressive and their display does sort of intrigue you. They have some interesting techniques and grips that seem to make it easier for them to lift super heavy stuff without hyperextending their wrists. Good to know.

They continue to try to outdo each other, swapping one large weight for an even larger one, and then an even larger one. One of the guys must have noticed that you've been glancing their way and he asks you if you want to join their little challenge.

What do you do?

A. Say hell yes, then proceed to show off your mad skills. You can totally outdo them.

B. You give it a try for a couple reps, then leave the guys to do their thing.

C. You blush and say no thank you, then scurry to another part of the gym, embarrassed you were caught staring.

D. You say you're impressed with their skills, but you wouldn't want to intrude on their competition.

E. You say yes, but that you're pretty sure you wouldn't be able to compete strength-wise—which is the honest truth.

F. Would you really be at the gym working out? In the slim case that you are, you'd decline the offer to participate but ask if you could watch so you can study their skills.

QUIZ #39

THE RUMOR

You're at home having dinner with your parents when your best friend sends you a super urgent text that you need to call her *right away*. You excuse yourself and give her a call—seriously, what could be so important?

Turns out that a girl at school has started an awful rumor about you. Basically, she's dating your ex-boyfriend (who you broke up with months ago) and she's obviously threatened by your presence, for reasons unknown. So, to turn others against you, she's made up a terrible story that paints you in a bad light.

Your best friend says she's been getting texts and social media messages all night from people asking if the rumor is true. She's been trying to field them, but she's worried that people actually believe this girl—and that your reputation might be at stake.

The situation is ridiculous: This girl should just be happy that she has a new boyfriend and leave it at that. The only reason you could think of to justify why she might want to hurt you is that because you and your ex are still friendly—she may be concerned that he may want you back at some point. So, her insecurity is now costing you your good name.

What do you do?

A. You talk to your ex and tell him he needs to fix the situation.

B. You don't want any trouble, so you just ignore the whole situation until it blows over.

C. You confront her and demand that she stops spreading lies about you. You're fully capable of making her keep her mouth shut, if needed, and you want her to know that.

D. Making a big deal out of it may just make people think the rumor's true after all—you try reverse psychology and pretend it doesn't bother you.

E. You think people should know the truth, so you defend yourself on Twitter and Facebook, clearing your name.

F. You fight back by being overly nice to her. Clearly, someone who makes up lies about other people is very sad inside, and you kind of feel sorry for her.

QUIZ #40

THE AFTER-SCHOOL FIGHT

There's a major situation happening at school today. One of the upperclassmen threw some really offensive insults toward a lowerclassman's sister, and rumor has it that the two boys are set to fight after school.

Everyone is talking about what's being called The Fight, as if it's some kind of sporting event. People are even taking bets on who's going to win. Your school is rather tame and passive—you've never heard of or seen anyone physically battle it out before, which is why this is such a big deal.

Apparently, the upperclassman has been taunting the younger guy for a whole month now about his sister (who is quite attractive), his hair (which is not attractive), and his lisp (which is just plain rude). The lowerclassman has had it at this point, and he's the one who suggested that they "take it outside."

The final bell rings and everyone rushes to the grass behind the bleachers where the fight is set to take place. The crowd organizes into an oval to clear a ring and the boys find their way to the center, fists raised. They slowly circle each other a few times, spitting insults until someone throws the first punch.

What do you do?

A. You leave before the action starts—you don't like violence.

B. You walk into the middle and try to convince both parties that they shouldn't fight each other.

C. You document the event on your phone so you have evidence of what actually happened, just in case.

D. You want to say or do something that will stop the fight, but you also don't want to get involved.

E. You make sure you're right on the edge of the circle. You may even step in if the weaker of the two boys needs a second.

F. You've never seen a fight before, so you're curious to watch how this plays out. You stay in the back, though, to be cautious.

QUIZ #41

THE COSTUME PARTY

Checking your e-mail one morning, you see a Paperless Post invite for a party. You click on the invitation and, to your surprise, you see that you've been invited to the coolest guy in school's annual Halloween party—which is pretty much an honor, given that not everyone gets asked to attend. This is the first year your name has made the list.

The party is still a couple weeks away (you were just asked to Save the Date in the invite), so you have some time to figure out your costume. You've heard that people tend to go all out for this shindig, which means that you really want to mull over what to wear: Do you want to look like you belong there? Do you want to stand out? Do you want to be cute, or scary? Did your crush get invited, too? (If so, that might change everything.)

Your browse Pinterest for costume ideas, debating among options that feature movie-caliber makeup, super scandalous getups, and clever DIYs. You want your costume to be unique enough so that it's not something everyone is wearing.

Finally, you settle on what you're going to dress up as for the party, after weighing all possibilities.

What do you choose?

A. You get some also-invited friends together, and make a group decision to wear costumes that are coordinating but tame, like Troll Dolls or cartoon characters.

B. You take this opportunity to wear something as scary as possible, and dress up like a decomposing zombie with plenty of fake blood.

C. You dress up like a pun or play on words, wearing a T-shirt that says "Life" on it and handing out lemons to everyone.

D. You dress up as something festive but generic, like a witch. You don't want to draw attention to yourself.

E. You think costume parties are kind of silly, because it's just about pretending to be someone you're not—you decide to just wear a fun wig or glasses.

F. You dress like your favorite TV character and hope that people get it.

QUIZ #42

THE COOL GIRLS

You've just been invited (so to speak) into the cool clique at school, and the whole group is headed to the local pool for a day of fun in the sun. You grab your best swimsuit, a color-coordinating towel, and your new sunglasses. Hanging with this group is pretty thrilling—you've never been in the popular crowd and you're curious to find out what it's really like. (And if the girls' perpetually amazing hair days will somehow transfer to you by association.)

You get to the pool and all the girls are gathered on a group of lounge chairs, chatting. You feel awkward, wondering if they're talking about you, but then they wave you over with smiles and hellos, patting a seat for you to fill. You could get used to this, feeling accepted by those who you admire.

The girls seem to be debating something; an initiation, it seems, because that word keeps coming up. You interject when the moment's right and ask what they're talking about. One of the girls, the leader of the group, turns to you and says that, in order to be fully "in" the clique, you have to jump off the high diving board and prove your worth to everyone. Otherwise you'll have to leave immediately, and no one will ever speak to you again.

You're kind of shocked... and yet, isn't this what you expected from these girls? It couldn't be so simple that they wanted to be friends just because they liked you—there had to be a catch.

What do you do?

A. It doesn't make sense to be friends with people who do this sort of thing, so you tell them thanks, but no thanks; you'll find other friends.

B. You don't want to be ostracized or cause conflict, so you go along with it.

C. You ask the girls what they had to do to earn their entrances into the group.

D. If it really means that much to them, sure, you'll just do it.

E. These "friends" sound like they aren't really nice people, so you tell them that and end your relationship with them.

F. *Pssht.* You're not afraid to make a silly old high-dive. You walk right over, climb the seemingly endless ladder, and leap off, startling the group with your bravery. You figure that you'll decide later if you actually want to be friends with these people anymore.

QUIZ #43

THE RELATION-SHIP DEAL BREAKER

You're dating a new guy, and you think this one has serious long-term potential. Okay, it's only been three months and you know you're still in that so-called honeymoon phase of the relationship, but you really, truly like him. He's sweet, smart, funny—and he laughs at your jokes. Your friends like him. Your family likes what they've heard about him so far. Everything seems great.

However, there have been a few red flags along the way, some bumps in the road that indicate that maybe he's not the right person for you for the long haul. That's okay—every person (and every relationship) has imperfections. You're never going to find someone that checks off all of your boxes, right?

So you keep dating and getting to know each other better. And then, one day, you realize that you could never, ever, ever permanently be with the guy. You two are out together when a bomb totally drops, and the situation changes everything you thought you knew about the guy. There is no way, no how, you could ever be with him in any serious capacity. (And thank goodness you learned this sooner rather than later, right?)

What happened that made you change your mind about him?

A. He said he was at home with his parents for a "family night"—you later found out that he was out with the boys. Lying is not cool in your book.

B. He told you he still keeps in touch with his ex-girlfriend. Fine. What he didn't tell you is that they still get coffee once a week. Not sharing key information? Not okay.

C. He got in a fight with some random guy. Yes, the other guy started it, but you don't want to be with someone who would needlessly fight back like that.

D. You told him it's your dream to go on a hot air balloon ride. He said he's too scared to even fly in an airplane. You need to be with someone who can share all of life's adventures with you.

E. Honestly, it's not something tangible that you can put your finger on, just more of an internal feeling that something isn't right.

F. A homeless man asked for the guy's leftovers when you two came out of a restaurant, and he said no. Seriously, who does that?

QUIZ #44

THE SNOW DAY

You wake up in the morning and, to your surprise and delight, the world outside is all white. Frost encrusts your bedroom window, and the sky is flecked with millions of snowflakes.

You head into the kitchen, and outside the window you see piles and piles of fresh snow on the ground. Excited, you log into your e-mail to see if there are any updates from school, perhaps a mass message saying that it's closed for the day.

Sure enough, at 5:55 A.M., there's the glorious message you seek: It's a snow day! No classes for you.

The snow outside is high, but you think it's soft enough to shovel. You get to work making a path out of the driveway so you're not stuck at home. Your mom offers you her car, as long as you drop her off and pick her up at work. (Adults don't get snow days, apparently.)

You have a vehicle and the next eight hours to yourself, to do whatever you please. Yes, it's still snowing. And it's cold. But your possibilities are almost limitless—and all of your friends are free to hang out, too.

What do you do with your unexpected free day?

A. You spend half the day with your friends, and half the day catching up on your chores so you can get your allowance before the weekend.

B. You and your friends play in the snow, making snow angels, then bake some pies and drink hot chocolate at someone's house.

C. You use the time to deliver food and blankets to homeless people, then head to the local library to mentor kids in reading.

D. It feels dishonest to go out when school's closed. You do a daytime sleepover with your BFFs; you guys stay in your PJs, pop popcorn, and play Truth or Dare.

E. You and your friends make an epic snow obstacle course, then challenge each other to see who can get through it the fastest.

F. You have a test tomorrow, so you use the time to get in some extra studying. Then you watch that science documentary you've been dying to see.

QUIZ #45

THE WALLET

You're browsing in a men's clothing store, shopping for a gift. It's a very high-end store and you can't afford most of what's in here, but you want to get your dad something nice for his birthday. Your budget is only $100, and most items in here cost more than $200.

As you sort through the ties, looking for one that's halfway decent-looking and on sale, you spot something that doesn't belong. It's a wallet, and it looks like someone accidentally left it behind while shopping.

The wallet itself is super nice. It's soft black leather with an embossed insignia. It probably cost a couple of hundred dollars just on its own. You look inside and it's chock-full of cash—at least $400 in bills. There are also a couple of blank checks and five credit cards.

You pull out the ID and recognize the name of a high-powered businessman in your town. You actually spotted him coming out of the store as you went in. The guy probably wouldn't even care if his wallet went missing—he has more than enough money. If you were to keep the wallet, no harm would likely come to you; there's no way he would go looking for it; he would just buy another one and consider the cash a (small) loss.

What do you do?

A. Leave the wallet right where it is. You don't want to be responsible for it.

B. Mail the wallet back with a note—hey, maybe you'll get a reward.

C. Using the address on the ID, you mail the wallet back to the man anonymously, at your own expense.

D. Give it to the woman behind the cash register so she can keep it safe until the owner returns for it.

E. You run out of the store, wallet in hand, to catch up to the guy (not thinking that, if he already realized that he lost his wallet, someone running with it is going to look pretty suspicious).

F. Turn it in to the police station—that's the most secure place for it.

QUIZ #46

THE SECRET

You've been invited to participate in a very hush-hush game that involves winning an enormous sum of money with little effort on your part. You're not a material person, but the prospect of some unexpected cash appeals to you because your family isn't well off; your parents both work very hard to keep a roof over your head and food on the table. Any chance you can take extra shifts at your afterschool job or do work for neighbors, you take it.

This amount of money, however, changes everything: You have the chance to win at least $10,000.

But here's the catch: To win the money, you must divulge your deepest, darkest secret to everyone you know. You must put up whatever it is as a social media post, so that literally everyone can see it. And if you lie, and the people running this game find out, you will have to pay a fine of double the money that you won dishonestly.

The more embarrassing or humiliating or shaming the secret is, the more money you can receive in this game. You can't tell a secret about another person, only yourself. And you can't lie—that is, unless you want to financially ruin your family.

You can, of course, decide not to play and walk away from this game without any consequences befalling you. But this opportunity will never come around again.

Do you play the game?

A. If the money will help your family, you decide it's worth it. You put up something that won't shame your family, but could win you a good amount of money.

B. You have no shame—you post your worst secret and collect your cash.

C. You're more curious about seeing what others put up than collecting money, so you decline. Plus, a terrible secret might ruin your future political career.

D. You're conflicted, so you ask your family for advice on what you should do.

E. You're not afraid of being made fun of, and you're pretty sure that people are too intimidated by you to even try. You play.

F. Money isn't everything. You feel like this game will just lead to people shaming each other, so you don't take part.

QUIZ #47

THE CATCALL

It's a gorgeous spring day and you're walking down the street, window shopping and soaking up the sun in a cute little area of town near your house. You're enjoying some "me time," just having a couple hours to yourself with nowhere to be and no one to talk to.

You're wearing a swingy red dress that makes you feel amazing, and you're having a great hair day. It's one of those moments when you feel like life is brimming with possibility and you're excited to be alive.

After browsing in a couple shops and grabbing a latte, you decide you'd better go home and start making plans for the evening. You fumble in your purse to check your phone for the time while you walk, wanting to see if your best friend texted you about that party she was thinking about going to tonight.

In the midst of your mental multitasking, you must have forgotten to take that right turn to your house because you've walked down a block you're unfamiliar with. There's a row of old, practically crumbling houses, and one of them has a construction crew outside, working high up on scaffolding. There's a group of ten or so men covered in dust, huddled together on the sidewalk, right where you're headed. It's too late to turn around or cross the street, so you walk right through them. You clutch your phone in your hand, just in case.

One of the guys lets out a loud whistle and says, "Hey there, baby, where are you headed off to so fast? Why don't you stay here with us?" His voice makes your skin crawl.

What do you do?

A. Inform him that his behavior is predatory and threatening, and that he should stop calling out to women on the street if he doesn't want to be perceived as a creep.
B. Say thank you and smile at him, walking quickly.
C. Growl in his direction and ask him if he wants to get punched in the face.
D. Inform him that technically, you are not, in fact, a "baby," and that he should think twice before he speaks, so as to not sound unintelligent.
E. Duck your head and pretend you didn't hear him.
F. Glare at him but say nothing.

QUIZ #48

THE FRENEMIES

There's a group made up of what can only be described as "mean girls" at school. They're always fighting (with each other), starting drama (with everyone else), and causing a total rift among basically all the other girls in your grade. They start rumors, make each other cry, and cause tension wherever they go. No one likes to be around them, and while they technically aren't breaking school rules with their behavior, they are causing situation after situation, and it needs to stop.

You and your friends try to stay away from this toxic clique, but sometimes one or two of their members will come sit with your group at lunch when their own table is getting too dramatic.

Because they can be disruptive in class and to other students, the higher-ups at the school are now getting involved to try to get to the bottom of the situation and finally answer the question: What's with these girls?

Since you're the president of the student council, the guidance counselor calls you in to talk about this situation—she needs someone who is impartial (as in, not great friends with anyone in the group, but not enemies with anyone, either) to explain to her why they can't stop fighting among themselves—and why they are so rude to other people.

What do you think the problem is? What would cause a group of friends to act like this?

A. The girls aren't honest with each other—or themselves—so they end up backstabbing each other instead.

B. The girls aren't kind to each other, so they constantly hurt each other's feelings and cause bad blood.

C. The girls have so many issues, you don't even know where to begin.

D. The girls are too self-involved—they just care about their own self-interests and they ignore everyone else's.

E. The girls don't know how to be good friends, and they're not curious to learn what it means to be one.

F. The girls are cowardly; they don't stick up for someone when she is being singled out or marginalized; they just set others against her.

QUIZ #49

THE ALIEN INVASION

Earth has just received a signal from outer space. There is an alien ship that wants permission to break through our atmosphere and establish face-to-face contact with our world leaders. They say they are from a place light-years upon light-years away. In fact, they have been traveling more than 250 years to find our planet, which seems almost inconceivable.

We know little about these extraterrestrials, save for the fact that they want to meet with us and have journeyed very long and very far to do so. But, curious about the possibility of other life (and not wanting to make them mad), we agree to let them land their ship. The U.N. decides that the United States is the best possible place for the meeting to happen.

The aliens will land in one hour. The meeting will be broadcast on every major channel around the globe, and translated into every language. The whole world will be watching this moment, which marks a rare instance of solidarity. Today, we are humans of the Earth, not fragmented by the boundaries of religion, race, or nationality.

You are the Secretary of State; as our nation's diplomat concerned with foreign affairs, you are the one who will greet the aliens and determine the reason they've traveled to meet us. You've been strategizing a plan of action for this historic event.

What is your intention for this first alien meeting?

A. Try to communicate with them.
B. Try to help them, or see if they come seeking help.
C. Try to befriend them.
D. Try to figure out if they come in peace—if not, you've got your army poised to attack.
E. Try to radiate peace to make them feel comfortable, while also trying to determine their true intentions.
F. Try to determine if they are trustworthy.

QUIZ #50

THE TEACUP

Your mom has an amazing teacup collection. On one cold winter day, you decide it would be a really good idea to make yourself a hot cup of tea and use one of her dainty cups to drink it from.

Now, your mom has told you many, many times how much she values this collection. And because each teacup is so fragile, she's asked you to please not touch them. A request that, until today, you've followed religiously.

But you're older now (and more careful, you presume), so you think that, just this once, you'll use a teacup. You'll drink from it, then you'll wash it carefully, and put it back. No harm done.

You brew your tea and pour it into a pink and silver teacup—your mom's favorite one. You sit at the kitchen table and sip your tea lightly, taking extra care to set the cup down gently after each sip. See? Totally fine.

Your tea finished, you get up and start to wash the cup in the sink, coating it with warm water, then hand soaping it. The soap is slippery but you hold firm. Once or twice the teacup almost slips from your grasp, but you don't let it hit the sink.

Finally, you go to dry it off with the kitchen towel when the phone rings suddenly, causing you to lose concentration—and your grip. The teacup falls straight onto the kitchen tile, breaking into pieces.

What do you do?

A. You wouldn't have used the teacup in the first place—Mom told you not to.
B. You put the broken pieces in your dresser drawer and hope that she doesn't notice.
C. You tell her right away, knowing full well that there may be consequences.
D. You tell her that you accidentally broke it—she knows you can be clumsy when it comes to delicate things.
E. You research the teacup maker and year that cup was made, and search eBay for the exact same one so you can replace it.
F. You feel conflicted for days over what you should do, then you decide to come clean.

SCORING

Now that you have completed your Aptitude Test, it's time to determine your score—and, more importantly, your faction!

Using the score sheet here, carefully circle the answer choice you selected for each question of your test. Each answer choice corresponds to a specific number. Once you have selected all of your answers, total up the numbers you have circled to get your official score and record your score at the bottom of the score sheet.

Look at the score results to see where your number falls and what faction you belong in.

Score Sheet

	POINTS FOR ANSWERS					
QUIZ #	A	B	C	D	E	F
Quiz #1	4	2	12	6	8	10
Quiz #2	10	6	8	2	12	4
Quiz #3	12	4	2	8	10	6
Quiz #4	10	4	6	8	12	2
Quiz #5	8	4	6	10	2	12

POINTS FOR ANSWERS

QUIZ #	A	B	C	D	E	F
Quiz #6	2	12	4	8	6	10
Quiz #7	10	6	8	4	12	2
Quiz #8	6	4	12	2	8	10
Quiz #9	8	4	6	12	2	10
Quiz #10	6	8	4	2	10	12
Quiz #11	12	4	8	6	10	2
Quiz #12	2	4	8	10	12	6
Quiz #13	2	12	4	10	6	8
Quiz #14	6	4	12	2	8	10
Quiz #15	6	10	8	4	12	2
Quiz #16	12	6	8	10	4	2
Quiz #17	8	4	2	6	12	10
Quiz #18	8	12	6	2	4	10
Quiz #19	4	6	2	8	10	12
Quiz #20	6	4	2	12	10	8
Quiz #21	8	6	12	4	2	10
Quiz #22	12	2	6	4	8	10
Quiz #23	4	2	8	10	12	6

POINTS FOR ANSWERS

QUIZ #	A	B	C	D	E	F
Quiz #24	2	6	4	8	10	12
Quiz #25	10	12	8	4	2	6
Quiz #26	6	10	2	12	8	4
Quiz #27	10	8	6	2	12	4
Quiz #28	12	6	10	8	4	2
Quiz #29	10	4	6	8	2	12
Quiz #30	8	2	12	4	10	6
Quiz #31	10	12	8	2	4	6
Quiz #32	10	2	6	12	4	8
Quiz #33	12	8	10	2	6	4
Quiz #34	2	4	8	6	12	10
Quiz #35	4	8	10	2	6	12
Quiz #36	4	12	2	10	8	6
Quiz #37	2	10	8	6	12	4
Quiz #38	8	12	4	2	6	10
Quiz #39	12	4	8	10	6	2
Quiz #40	4	2	6	12	8	10
Quiz #41	4	8	10	2	6	12

	POINTS FOR ANSWERS					
QUIZ #	A	B	C	D	E	F
Quiz #42	10	4	12	2	6	8
Quiz #43	6	10	4	8	12	2
Quiz #44	12	4	2	6	8	10
Quiz #45	4	12	2	10	8	6
Quiz #46	2	6	10	12	8	4
Quiz #47	6	2	8	10	4	12
Quiz #48	6	4	12	2	10	8
Quiz #49	10	2	4	8	12	6
Quiz #50	2	4	6	8	10	12

Total Score: _____

If you scored between 100 and 149 points, you're in **Abnegation**. Check out Faction Breakdown #1 in Part 2 to learn more.

If you scored between 150 and 249 points, you're in **Amity**. Check out Faction Breakdown #2 in Part 2 to learn more.

If you scored between 250 and 349 points, you're in **Candor**. Check out Faction Breakdown #3 in Part 2 to learn more.

If you scored between 350 and 449 points, you're in **Dauntless**. Check out Faction Breakdown #4 in Part 2 to learn more.

If you scored between 450 and 549 points, you're in **Erudite**. Check out Faction Breakdown #5 in Part 2 to learn more.

If you scored between 550 and 600 points, you're among the rarest of the rare, **Divergent**. Check out Faction Breakdown #6 in Part 2 to learn more.

PART 2

DISCOVER YOUR FACTION

Now that you've finished scoring your Aptitude Test and you know which faction you belong to, it's time to delve deeper into your ideal faction. In this section, you will learn what your faction's lifestyle might be like in real life, if the world within the Divergent universe was a little more like our world of today.

Each Faction Breakdown—even including Divergent—will take you through facets of your personality and your life within your faction, and will include information on your favorite activities, your job, your friendships, your family life, your romantic outlook, and so on.

While the Faction Breakdowns are meant to correspond with your Aptitude Test score, there's certainly no harm in taking a peek at all of the factions' sections to better understand them as a whole. Use this part of the book not only to discover new information (and to reinforce what you might already suspect) about yourself, but to also uncover fun details about other people as well. Perhaps your best friend or sibling scored into a different faction than you—and wouldn't it be fun to better comprehend his or her core characteristics as well as your own?

So, without further ado, flip to your Faction Breakdown and see how your test score matches up to the real you.

FACTION BREAKDOWN 1
ABNEGATION

Ah, Abnegation: selfless, always thinking of others. Without you, who would reach a hand out to a friend in need, give some change to a hungry homeless person, or share kind words with the school outcast?

Above all else, you value altruism. But not because of the fuzzy feeling you may get for your good deeds or because you want recognition from other people. No, your self-effacing personality is simply *you*: You help others because you couldn't imagine *not* helping others. Which, as far as ingrained traits go, is a pretty good one to have. Here's how life would be—and who you would be—as a true member of Abnegation.

> **A FEW OF YOUR FAVORITE THINGS**
>
> **Favorite color:** Gray
>
> **Role model:** Oprah Winfrey
>
> **Favorite movie or TV show:** Extreme Makeover: Home Edition
>
> **Favorite guilty pleasure:** Sneaking a glance of yourself in the mirror
>
> **Favorite room in your house:** The kitchen, where you're typically found cooking for your family
>
> **Favorite holiday:** Thanksgiving
>
> **Favorite possession:** Well, material things aren't that important to you, but you would probably choose your watch if you had to pick something

YOUR PERSONALITY

THE UPSIDE

Your giving nature makes you anything but self-centered. You're grounded and realistic about life—you're not one to take things lightly, but you're also not overdramatic. People often think of you as self-sufficient since you never seem to focus on yourself. (If you're stressed or worried about something, you tend to keep it inside rather than blab on and on about whatever is making you anxious.)

You're also very patient. You see overeagerness and irritation as forms of selfishness, which is why you are quite skilled at tolerating both tiresome tasks and people.

Another one of your core values is respect. You respect other people's space, property, ideas, values—you name it. You're also a rule follower and rarely get in trouble. After all, if you were to act up, you would just end up being a burden to others.

THE DOWNSIDE

Because you're always trying to do the right thing, you can come off a bit goody two-shoes or even as someone who's holier than thou. While it's great to play life by the book, being too rigid may cause you to miss out on some fun. And even though giving back to others is admirable, beware of being too charitable: Less kind people tend to take advantage of those who always give, give, give. Plus, at some point you do need to think about yourself and your needs. You don't want to use your giving nature as a crutch to avoid thinking—or taking action—about issues in your own life.

YOUR STYLE

No one would ever describe you as vain, that's for sure. "No fuss, no muss" is practically your personal mantra when it comes to fashion and style. You'll always choose comfort and practicality over the latest sartorial sensation.

In the Divergent universe, people within the Abnegation faction are mandated to wear drab gray robes day after day after day. In our world, those probably wouldn't fly. Still, your fashion sense isn't so far removed from that classic, "stiff" attire. For you, comfort is key, as is not calling too much attention to yourself. Therefore, your style consists mainly of classics like jeans and gray T-shirts paired with no-nonsense shoes. Neon colors, rhinestone details, and acid-washed jeans are *so* not for you.

As far as hair and makeup go, your preference is similarly low-key. Buns, ponytails, and easy braids are Abnegation women's go-to styles. If you do wear makeup, you probably tend to stick with the basics: powder, mascara, and lip gloss. And getting manicures? *Please*. Who wants to sit in a chair for an hour to have someone buff your nails? Your time is better spent elsewhere.

YOUR ACTIVITIES AND HOBBIES

Volunteering is, of course, your number one way to spend your free time. Even if you don't have much time to spare, you always find ways to do something for others. In fact, you may even spend school breaks or holidays devoting yourself to those in need, doing anything from building houses in South America to serving food at a shelter on Thanksgiving Day. For you, it's not so much about what you're doing as it is about who you're doing it for.

Your other hobbies, while enjoyable because they help you unwind, also typically serve others. Because you value things that are handmade—more special than store-bought, right?—you like to get crafty and handy with hobbies like sewing and woodworking. Since you're so patient, you can pull off creating intricate designs without driving yourself crazy or giving up. You usually give your creations to friends and family to make those around you feel special and thought of.

When it comes to sports, you prefer to be a spectator rather than a player. Your selfless predilection doesn't make you very competitive. Because watching relatively violent games can bother you, you prefer watching no-contact games like tennis over football and basketball any day.

As far as the arts go, you have a deep appreciation for people whose talent exceeds your own (which, because you're so humble, is basically everyone). Whether you're watching a professional ballet company or a community theatre performance, you'll be the audience member who claps the loudest, wanting to encourage the artists putting on a show.

YOUR WORK LIFE

In the Divergent universe, Abnegation is the faction involved in the government—the idea being that those in charge should be selfless and only think of others. Of course, in the real world, that's not how things work. So, rather than being pigeonholed into one set career path, there are actually a number of jobs you would be great for.

Given your love for charity, running your own non-profit—or just working for one—is a great option for you. Because you are patient and deeply invested in others, teaching would also be quite fulfilling, as you get to play a role in nurturing the next generation. Working as a public defender could also be an interesting career path for you, as you would get to take on cases for people who sometimes have no one else to step up for them and their rights.

As an employee, you're a valuable member of any team because you're not after your own self-interests: You put the company as a whole, your colleagues, and the goals at hand ahead of your own agenda. (Wait, what agenda? You never seem to have one.) Each contribution you make is for the greater good, and helps you and your team achieve a common goal.

But while your selfless efforts in the workplace won't go unnoticed, you may need to ease up on always thinking of others when it comes time to ask for a much-deserved raise or move on to another company. A fear of being selfish or letting others down may keep you from reaching your true potential, so make sure that your desire to always serve others doesn't end up hurting your career in the long run.

YOUR FRIENDSHIPS

In theory, you would be a wonderful friend. Because you put others first, you are an excellent listener who would always have time to attend to a pal's relationship drama or lend a shoulder for your BFF to cry on. And people would trust you because you're also a great secret keeper—gossiping is completely self-serving and not very nice, in your opinion.

However, a true friendship can't be all give and no take. Your predisposition for listening patiently while other people spill their guts—but never divulging anything personal about yourself—can actually lead people to mistrust you and even feel awkward around you, which is likely the opposite of what you might want for them.

Another issue that could come up in your platonic relationships is that you tend to keep negative feedback or comments to yourself, not wanting to hurt a friend's feelings by telling him or her the truth. It's important for you to find a balance between being candid with your friends and being kind—these qualities aren't always as at odds as you might think.

YOUR LOVE LIFE

When it comes to romance, Abnegation's giving nature wins you major points. Since you're always involved in some volunteering project, you're always meeting new people who value altruism and care about others—qualities that are extremely important to you in an ideal mate.

You really make an effort to understand your partner, comfort him when needed, and try to attend to his wishes and wants. You're the partner that your boyfriend's friends wish they were dating because of the way you dote on him.

While your desire to make your partner as happy as can be is admirable, healthy relationships require give and take. Being the giver all the time doesn't allow your partner to take on that role and understand the joy of making *you* feel special and loved. Plus, constantly giving—and perhaps not getting as much in return—may end up breeding disdain over time. It's rare that someone can give and give and give and never expect anything in return, no matter how selfless she is. So do what you can to gracefully let your partner spoil you every once in a while.

One thing you're not so great at in relationships? Being affectionate. It's kind of an Abnegation thing to shy away from physical contact, but doing so may make your partner wonder if you're really that into him. Of course, you don't have to force yourself to be down with over-the-top PDA, but a little hand-holding while strolling the town never hurt anyone, right?

YOUR FAMILY LIFE

Growing up in an Abnegation family, you probably watched your parents constantly help others, and they encouraged you to do the same. Your family likely also values working together as a unit. If someone cooks, the others clean the dishes. Chores around the house are also divided up fairly, no matter who is older or younger, who is male or female, who is the parent or the child. In this way, you were taught egalitarian values when it comes to the household, and you likely shun the traditional (and outdated) model of women doing all the housework and childrearing.

While you and your kin strive to serve other people and treat each other fairly, your own family life can feel a touch tense at times. You don't tend to outright fight with your parents or siblings—it would be selfish and rude to talk back or bicker—but keeping your emotions under wraps does tend to brew underlying stress thanks to all the things left unsaid. But, all in all, you grew up happy and proud of your family: You knew your parents were good people and you respected the fact that they groomed you to be the same.

Peace loving, tree-hugging Amity—how can you be so kind? Easygoing, sweet, and giving, you rarely get riled up and, in the rare case you do, your anger quickly melts away.

Always the neutral party, you prefer to avoid conflicts of any kind—you think it's better to chill out rather than take sides. Which, naturally, might put off those who are rather opinionated. In fact, your "no worries" personality can make some people question how you stay so calm and collected, no matter what's at stake. But you're not bothered by any judgment call made at your expense (of course). Read on to discover how being Amity might play out in the real world.

A FEW OF YOUR FAVORITE THINGS

Color: Red or yellow

Role model: John Lennon

Movie or TV show: *SpongeBob SquarePants*

Guilty pleasure: Eating freshly picked apples

Room in your house: Family room, where you can spend time with loved ones

Holiday: Earth Day

Possession: Valuing things is silly—love is all you need

YOUR PERSONALITY

THE UPSIDE

Your accepting nature inspires you to always strive for mutual understanding with other people, allowing you to see the good in every person or situation. Being optimistic is simply your default—you never assume others have bad intentions or ulterior motives, and you continually look on the bright side.

You're an open person who likes to greet others with a friendly embrace. Sure, this might put people who value their personal space off, but it's hard for others to take offense at your constant cheerfulness and warmth.

Being nice to others just feels right to you. In your opinion, there's always space in your heart for one more friend or one more opportunity to be kind. The phrase "turn the other cheek" also comes to mind when describing you and your faction-mates. You just don't see the point in being mean to others, even if they have wronged or hurt you.

Another core value of yours is an affinity toward being polite. You are big on social niceties—not because you want to impress people or make others think highly of you—but because graciousness comes easily to you.

THE DOWNSIDE

There are always going to be those people who are suspicious of someone who's happy and kind all the time. You may find yourself up against hostility from others who don't understand that your kindness isn't a front. That said, being continually optimistic and good-natured does seem a bit, well, unrealistic. You may find yourself repressing negative emotions (consciously or unconsciously) and, at some point, those may blow up.

YOUR STYLE

In the world of Divergent, Amity people dress casually and comfortably in red and yellow. In our real world, this isn't always possible or desirable. (Maybe you're not a fan of those colors.) Given your peace, love, and happiness vibes, you're likely drawn to boho or hippie-inspired clothing, and tend to wear bright, loose-fitting pieces that make you feel happy and free.

To put others at ease, you likely shy away from in-your-face graphic T-shirts that make political statements or any kind of clothing that might make others uncomfortable. Same with your hair; you keep your 'do simple and easy, no faux-hawks, dreads, or half-shaven styles for your tresses.

When it comes to your makeup, when you wear it, it's fresh and pretty—you sometimes brush on a little blush to emphasize your cheeks and some shiny lip gloss to highlight your smile.

YOUR ACTIVITIES AND HOBBIES

For fun, you enjoy non-competitive games like Psychiatrist (in which one person plays a doctor, one acts out the part of a patient, and everyone else asks the doctor questions to guess the patient's affliction) and group storytelling, where everyone is involved and there are no winners or losers. Traditional sports get too competitive, plus there's that terrible process of choosing teams, which ends up making those who aren't as strong or skilled feel badly about themselves.

Amity people tend to be lovers of the arts, especially music. Attending outdoor concerts, drum circles, and group sing-alongs are some of your favorite ways to unwind and bond with others. But you appreciate any type of artistic endeavor, as long as it has a community spirit and isn't elitist.

Because, in the Divergent universe, Amity focuses on harvesting the people's food, you may also enjoy gardening and cooking with foods you cultivate from your own backyard. You're a born nurturer so taking care of plants, and then feeding others with them, is a full-circle, feel-good activity for you. Or, even if you don't have a green thumb, you may just enjoy heading to a local farm for some apple picking every now and then.

YOUR WORK LIFE

In addition to being harvesters, some members of the Amity faction serve as caregivers. In our world, you have many, many more choices for your career path instead of just these two.

Your kind nature lends itself well toward working as a kindergarten teacher, running a summer camp, or daycare, as children will be naturally drawn to your free spirit and happy demeanor.

Because you care so much about peace, especially between large groups of people, you would make an excellent UN ambassador, missionary, or world peace activist. Your passion for equality and harmony will easily shine through and come across as authentic.

In the workplace, your smile sets others at ease and helps foster a sense of community among your team members. You come into the office with a positive vibe and ready to take on the day, inspiring your coworkers to brighten up a little, too. Because you refuse to let anything or anyone get you down, you take criticism in stride and setbacks as only temporary inconveniences.

Sometimes your ability to maintain your happiness can come off as if you don't really care, or might even be a little bit, well, unintelligent, to be frank. But you don't let other people's opinions of your naturally kind state affect you. Your main goal is to create a peaceful workplace where others can thrive, and if people want to question your motives, that's their issue (and you feel for them).

YOUR FRIENDSHIPS

As a faction, Amity strongly values friendship, so of course you take your friendships very seriously. Friends are like family to you, and you protect their feelings and their hearts as if they were your own.

If your friends do quarrel, you never take sides. You remain a neutral party that helps the others work toward making up, which makes you a very valuable asset within your group. Your pals know they can count on you to restore the peace.

Your treat your friends delicately, never saying a harsh word, always delivering positive feedback and encouragement. At times this can backfire when a friend really wants your honest opinion on something, but if your opinion is negative, you truly will not give it. This can make your friendships less real, in a sense; while your friends never get angry with you and you always have fun hanging out, there's a layer of authenticity that might not be there, preventing true, deep friendships from solidifying.

It works best for you to have fellow Amities as your friends. This way, no one is bothered by—or suspicious of—the smooth-sailing nature of your friendships (and the fact that you've never once disagreed with a pal).

YOUR LOVE LIFE

In some ways, you are a dream romantic partner: You love and cherish your significant other and you never have a complaint about your relationship. You're always happy, never get angry, and always seem up for anything.

Yet, because you feel the need to maintain neutrality and never want to disappoint anyone, you have a hard time making decisions. If your boyfriend asks you where you want to go out for dinner, you always respond with "Wherever you want to go!" Which, at times, can be frustrating for him. Because you're always aiming to please and keep the peace, you can inadvertently cause tension—your partner may not believe that you really and truly do not have a preference.

When tensions do arise, though, you always know how to diffuse them with soothing words, conceding that getting angry is never worth it. Those who are looking for a passionate, fight-and-make-up sort of relationship should not look to you for a partner. You need someone who can take charge and steer the relationship (or else no one will ever make a decision on where to go for a meal!), but someone who is also mild-mannered like you.

YOUR FAMILY LIFE

Growing up, your household was filled with love and laughter; you, your parents, and your siblings lived together in harmony. Your mom and dad taught you how to keep your cool, even when someone insulted you or was combative, shaping you into the peacekeeper you are today.

There was likely no harsh discipline in your home, only calm discussion, which allows you to understand how to swiftly resolve conflict without yelling or tears. You and your siblings were kind to one another, never fighting over toys, clothes, or material things, and your parents taught you the value of showing one another respect for the greater good of the family.

Deep down, there may have been some resentment or rivalry, but you don't dwell on negative thoughts and feelings like those for too long, so they are forgotten in the recesses of your childhood memories.

The phrase "the truth and nothing but the truth" rules the Candor faction, permeating every part of your life, from your personality to your friendships to your career. You value honesty above all else, believing that the problems we face in our world largely come from people who don't value it. Duplicity, telling lies, sugarcoating—these acts are not only unfavorable in your opinion, but they're actually dangerous, shrouding the truth from our lives.

Because you see things in black and white, you find it easy to make judgment calls and decisions, but you tend to miss out on those gray areas of life. Not having any wiggle room can make you quite rigid at times, causing others to see you as unyielding, even unfeeling. Here's what your truth-telling Candor ways might mean for you in the current world.

A FEW OF YOUR FAVORITE THINGS

Color: Black and white

Role model: Abraham Lincoln (a.k.a. "Honest Abe")

Movie or TV show: *Pretty Little Liars*

Guilty pleasure: Catching people telling lies

Room in your house: The bathroom, where all truths and flaws are revealed

Holiday: April Fools' Day (because no one can fool you)

Possession: Your journal

YOUR PERSONALITY

THE UPSIDE

Telling it like it is can be tough for many people, but for you, being honest comes easy. Your commitment to always telling the truth may have ended up getting you in trouble when you were younger (and even sometimes now at your current age), but this never stopped you from fessing up when you did something wrong. This quality makes you trustworthy—others know that they can rely on you for an honest opinion or account, no matter what.

For you, dishonesty creates barriers between people: family members, friends, romantic partners, even strangers. That's why when someone you don't even know asks you how your day's going and it's been terrible, you say so. Better to be honest and let the person know than create a lie between you. (Plus, maybe you'll show her that it's okay to be candid about how things are going in her own life.)

Basically, the truth always comes out eventually, and you believe it's wiser to be direct rather than waste everyone's time by not telling it immediately. Your transparency can be uncanny—if not unbelievable at times—but your ability to show all parts of yourself (even the not-so-great ones) can actually inspire people to feel more secure with their own shortcomings.

THE DOWNSIDE

Of course, the truth can hurt sometimes. Because you're always telling people the absolute truth, you sometimes bruise egos and feelings, making some people wary of asking your opinion on anything ever again. Your particular brand of honesty can feel abrasive, even invasive, to those who are not used to it, especially when you call people out on their own lies.

YOUR STYLE

In the Divergent universe, people in the Candor faction stick to wearing only black and white, and tend to be pretty formal in their way of dress, with women wearing long skirts and men wearing black suits with white ties.

In the real world, however, this may not be possible, or even something you'd want to do. So, as a Candor in today's world, you'll likely wear whatever you feel is authentic to you. No following fleeting trends (unless you love them), or giving in to the latest must-have accessory just because everyone else has. For example, you're not going to buy fluffy boots better suited for arctic weather when you live in a temperate climate, even if every other girl at school is doing it. And you choose clothing that truly flatters you, because you're so honest with yourself. You're able to see your flaws clearly and determine what cuts and fits work best on your body type—and then you stick with those.

When it comes to hair, you're similarly true to yourself. You wear your hair in a style that works with your face and bone structure. While makeup can feel a bit like dishonesty—you're literally enhancing your looks with eyeliner and concealer—you enjoy the guilty pleasure of putting it on for special occasions.

YOUR ACTIVITIES AND HOBBIES

More than anything, you love to debate, as it's an opportunity to discover—and defend—the truth. You may be on your school's debate team, or simply spend your free time arguing with anyone willing to verbally spar with you. You also enjoy attending debates, as you see the ability to argue a point without resorting to dramatics or truth-bending to be a real art form. Most of the time, you also enjoy catching those who are debating in their falsehoods, an exercise that helps hone your keen body language–reading skills.

When it comes to sports, you're a team player who believes in following the rules of the game. But if someone cheats or tries to bend the rules, you're out. And the same goes for board games, another pastime you enjoy. If someone decides to play dirty, you quit right where you are. You can't engage in an activity that's tainted with deception, after all. So, it's important for you to play with fellow Candors or equally standup people for you to enjoy yourself in any kind of competitive activity.

YOUR WORK LIFE

You're best suited for a career that can perfectly utilize your truthfulness and serve the greater good in the process. Being part of the justice system as a lawyer or judge is an obvious path for you to follow. But other jobs like a surgeon, a military officer, a banker, or a police officer require people with sound moral compasses and the ability to be honest, no matter the circumstances. If none of these careers appeal to you, you could even become a modern-day philosopher, researching what truth really means (and perhaps also teaching others by becoming a philosophy professor).

One thing is for sure, though, no matter which professional path you choose: Your ability to be honest should win you major points at work. Your colleagues will respect you for always coming clean when it was you who made a major mistake. Your boss will respect you for your upfront opinion about your own shortcomings and even those of the goings-on within the place you work—she knows that, no matter what, you will give your true feelings about a policy, a deadline, or a potential client.

Surely, though, being honest won't always work in your favor. If the boss comes by and asks if you like her new blouse, and you tell her that it's hideous, you're not going to get any bonus points for your honesty there. And if you uncover corruption or untoward practices and rat someone out, that person will certainly not thank you for your candor. Always being honest is a tricky thing and when it comes to your career, depending on those around you, this quality can be valued or it can be seen as a liability.

YOUR FRIENDSHIPS

As a friend, you're the one who will tell a pal if you are actually mad at her, if she does indeed look good in those jeans, or if you do in fact think her new boyfriend is a total jerk. Your bluntness may not always be tactful or appreciated in the moment, but in the long run, your friends value you for candidly putting it all out there right away.

But for you, a friendship isn't a real friendship if *both* people can't be honest with each other. (Surprise, surprise, right?) You value those who not only can take your straight talk, but can also dish it right back to you.

One aspect of friendship that you're particularly good at is shutting down the rumor mill. You're not a gossip—you don't believe in spreading information if you're not completely sure it's true—and you swiftly put the kibosh on falsehoods others spread about your friends.

YOUR LOVE LIFE

As with your friendships, your honesty comes into play in a big way in your romantic relationships. You need a partner who understands your truth-telling ways, and loves you for them. This person also needs to be down for spending hours at a time debating and reasoning over current events or other issues you find intriguing.

Being straightforward actually enhances the dating process for you: When you're into someone, you tell him. When you're not feeling someone, you let him know. There's no game-playing, beating around the bush, or mixed signals. You either want to continue seeing someone or you don't. This helps keep you from wasting time on the wrong person, or dragging your feet when you're really, *really* into someone.

Your biggest relationship deal breaker, of course, is dishonesty. If your significant other lies to you, you'll be very tempted to end things right then and there. To you, lies are barriers to true intimacy—the more that pile up, the farther away two people get from each other.

YOUR FAMILY LIFE

Your Candor nature comes, naturally, from your parents. Growing up, your mom and dad were probably honest with you and your siblings about the reality of life, both the good and the bad. As a result, you developed a very balanced view of the world and the people around you. You didn't put your parents or teachers on pedestals; you accepted their humanity and their capacity for making mistakes.

You also learned from an early age not to lie to your parents. Instead, you were open with them about your activities and whereabouts and this fostered open communication within your family.

You and your siblings likely engaged in deep discussions growing up, but you rarely fought. While you may have hurt each other's feelings by being perhaps a bit too honest with one another, you also accepted and appreciated one another's commitment to telling the truth.

Ever-fierce Dauntless are rarely discouraged by a challenge. Thrill-seeking and courageous, you're someone others look up to—and maybe even fear—because of your devil-may-care attitude toward life.

For you, nothing is more important than being brave, no matter what obstacle you face. You grab life by the horns and don't dwell on uncomfortable emotions like doubt and panic. In fact, you see fear as an obstacle you must face head-on in order to grow and become stronger, and you like to encourage others to live with valor, too. For you, the world's problems would be easier to solve if people would just sack up and become a bit more thick-skinned and strong-willed. Read on to discover what being Dauntless could look like in the real world.

A FEW OF YOUR FAVORITE THINGS

Color: Black

Role model: Evel Knievel

Movie or TV show: American Ninja Warrior

Guilty pleasure: Going to the shooting range

Room in your house: Your room, where you can be alone

Holiday: Halloween

Possession: Your pocketknife

YOUR PERSONALITY

THE UPSIDE

You believe in being resilient, powerful, and—most of all—brave. Other people look to you as a beacon of strength and, when the going gets tough, your toughness can be contagious. You're talkative (quite loud, at times) and you don't believe in niceties or formalities. Your come-as-you-are, take-me-or-leave-me attitude shows that you have a very strong sense of self. You don't care what others think of you, and if they don't like your demeanor, your clothes, your face, or your tattoos or piercings (if you have any), you couldn't care less. And, yes, this can be a positive thing: You're authentic and you don't hide who you are to others. This encourages other people to be more real with you, as well.

THE DOWNSIDE

You can be a bit confrontational, which can make others uneasy around you. You're always ready for a fight and tend to be easily provoked. Patience is not a virtue you possess—you're a person of action. You need to be doing something or staying busy so you can feel useful, meaning that you rarely give your body and mind a break. You can also be super stubborn.

YOUR STYLE

Basically, this faction's fashion sense is about as in your face as you can get. Members of Dauntless typically rock tight, black clothes that show off their lean bodies and muscles. Think skinny jeans, muscle-Ts and formfitting sheath dresses—and nothing frilly. As a member of this faction, you might have—or plan on getting—a number of tattoos and piercings, decorating your body with a story of your life in ink and metal.

When it comes to hair, you may dye your locks crazy colors or even fashion your 'do into intricate braids, cornrows, or mohawks. Dauntless women tend to wear smoky black eyeliner to emphasize their features, too. It's a little dangerous and a little sultry at the same time.

YOUR ACTIVITIES AND HOBBIES

When it comes to what you do in your downtime, the more daring the better. If it's extreme, you'll probably want to try it. Bungee jumping, skydiving, ziplining... you name it. For you, the purpose of an activity should be to either prove your bravery or get a killer rush. Or perhaps to hone your skills; you likely enjoy a round or two of target practice at a shooting range or archery club, taking time to perfect your shot.

As far as sports go, you're rarely a spectator. However, your competitive nature makes you a poor team player (you can be a bit of a ball hog). That's why individual sports like snowboarding, heliskiing, and motocross appeal to you: You don't need to depend on others on your team; you just straight up compete with yourself.

You're not much of a fan of the arts in the traditional sense ... unless Muay Thai and karate count as art forms?

YOUR WORK LIFE

In the Divergent universe, Dauntless are the protectors of the city, guarding the walls and keeping the other factions safe from potential threats. In our world, however, there are a number of jobs that require your particular brand of bravery, like police officer, firefighter, or a member of the armed forces. Other life-risking jobs, from deep-sea fisherman to hostage negotiator, may also appeal to you.

On the job, you're always the one who volunteers for the toughest, most dangerous assignments. Which, typically, makes those around you grateful that they don't have to risk their lives doing whatever it is you've signed yourself up for this time. You may even inspire those around you to be stronger and braver—and you're more than willing to share your knowledge of fighting and weapon-work with those who seem worthy.

However, you're not the easiest person to work with because you can be quite abrasive, even rude, to people you deem cowardly or meek. Plus, you don't have many social graces to speak of, so your brusqueness definitely puts others off. But once people get to know you, they typically admire you for telling things like they are and not being one who placates others for the sake of not hurting their feelings. Being frank and direct can get you in trouble sometimes, but when it comes to business, these qualities are often quite redeeming.

YOUR FRIENDSHIPS

You would literally die for your friends. You're loyal and dependable in a crisis, and you're always there when someone needs defending. You believe in speaking up—and fighting for—those who can't fight for themselves, so having a friend like you comes in handy for those who aren't quite as bold as you are.

However, because you're so used to living with discomfort (powering through it, really), you aren't always aware of when you make others uncomfortable. This is why you may not have as many friends as you'd like—it takes true courage to be best pals with you, since you're always suggesting some risky adventure or taking on some crazy stunt. You can also be moody and brooding, especially if you fail at some kind of task or challenge. Not everyone is willing to go along for the ride and, if they are, they have to be super resilient and not take things personally.

YOUR LOVE LIFE

The traits that make you a devoted friend make you an equally loyal partner in a relationship. You're willing to do anything for the person you love, even if that means putting yourself in grave danger.

Being in a relationship with you can be pretty intense, if not nerve-wracking. You don't have a lot of regard for your own safety, which can make your boyfriend nervous, if not completely frustrated that you're willing to take so many constant risks. Your self-reliance also can make a partner feel expendable and not needed—it takes a strong person to not feel intimidated or insignificant around you.

You tend to attract suitors who are enthralled by your wild, will-not-be-tamed nature. Seeking a thrill, these potential mates are eager to see if they can keep up with you. (In many cases, they probably can't.) To meet your ideal partner, keep your eyes peeled the next time you're doing one of your extreme activities—chances are you'll find a fellow adrenaline junkie with whom you can concoct daredevilish plans. Your life together will be filled with adventure, meaning there's hardly ever a dull moment as you take on new challenges and seek new thrills as a twosome.

YOUR FAMILY LIFE

Growing up, your parents likely instilled in you the value of fearlessness. Family vacations may have been spent battling river rapids and camping in remote locales, helping you hone your survival skills and squash timidity. It wasn't always easy, of course, as kids are afraid of a lot of things (the dark, monsters under your bed, and so on), but you developed a thick skin early in your life—you had to.

You always thought your parents were invincible and it was awesome how your mom was just as tough as your dad—there was no outdated mom-as-delicate-housewife sort of vibe in your house. Your parents' strength gave you strength, and they inspired you to go out there and conquer the world.

However, getting approval for performing daring stunts did put you and your siblings against each other sometimes, as you all tried to outdo one another's latest crazy trick. More often that not, however, you guys encouraged each other to get braver and braver, forming a thick bond of loyalty to each other and your family. What didn't kill you indeed made you stronger.

FACTION BREAKDOWN 5
ERUDITE

The brains of the Divergent universe, Erudite is all about wisdom. The constant pursuit of knowledge may sound tiresome to those not within your faction, but you just can't get enough of new facts, theories, and ideas.

This is pretty cool, if you think about it . . . which you probably already have. Being smart and—more importantly—using those smarts for the good of society is quite an admirable goal. And rather than shy away from stereotypical nerddom, you simply jump right in and own it. Here's what life could be like for you as an Erudite in the real world.

A FEW OF YOUR FAVORITE THINGS

Color: Blue

Role model: Steve Jobs

Movie or TV show: Inception

Guilty pleasure: Playing Minecraft

Room in your house: Your office

Holiday: Geek Pride Day (celebrated on May 25)

Possession: Laptop

YOUR PERSONALITY

THE UPSIDE

You see the world as your oyster. There are countless books to be read, far-off places to visit, and interesting people to interview. You are curious about, well, everything, and often your thirst and excitement for knowledge is contagious. You are the one who got your classmates pumped about doing experiments in science class and looking forward to going on educational field trips. (Okay, at first they thought you were crazy, but your enthusiastic persistence totally won them over in the end.)

Knowledge may be power, as the common phrase goes, but you don't let your smarts go to your head (or at least, you try not to). You see learning as an opportunity to share with others, whether it's helping your BFF with her math homework or showing your parents your latest invention.

THE DOWNSIDE

While your heart is usually in the right place, you can be kind of a know-it-all sometimes, which can put others off. Rather than watch those around you make mistakes, you have a bad habit of overcorrecting them, which can cause people to label you as bossy. You truly mean well—why should someone struggle, if you can easily help them, right?—but you may want to consider letting people fail (and learn from it) rather than always stepping in.

YOUR STYLE

Whether you mean to or not, you totally dress the part with your geek chic style. You're often seen wearing your favorite color, blue, and you prefer dressing in business casual when you get the chance, which means lots of blouses and pencil skirts. If you wear glasses, you rock them with pride. If you have 20/20 vision, you not-so-secretly wish you needed to wear specs (and sometimes you do wear them, just with non-prescription lenses).

As for hair and makeup, you like to keep things looking professional, but you can be a touch eccentric in the grooming department, since you often don't want to waste your time on the upkeep when your minutes could be spent reading or on the computer. For example, you tend to like the effect of a sleek bob, but also may occasionally sport a messy bun when you don't want to take time away from your studies to actually do your hair. As for makeup, it's all about the classics, since you want to come off professional: Perfect eyeliner and a berry lip are your go-tos.

YOUR ACTIVITIES AND HOBBIES

When you're not reading books or consuming information on the Internet, you're often engaging in some kind of intellectual hobby. Model building is an especially rewarding pastime for you, as you get to practice your meticulousness. (You probably loved Lego as a kid.) You also enjoy building web programs and writing code, keeping on the forefront of today's technology.

Playing games in which you need to use your mind can also be a fun escape from learning. You enjoy chess, Risk, Monopoly, and other challenging games of skill.

You're not great at sports—people often pick you last for teams because you're kind of labeled as a geek—but you can hold your own by combating all that brawn with your brain. And while you can intellectually appreciate the arts, they aren't exactly your thing, either. You'd rather go to a lecture by an astrophysicist than attend the ballet.

YOUR WORK LIFE

Erudite members are the record keepers in the Divergent universe, as well as the city's librarians, doctors, scientists, and teachers. But, of course, in our world, people of any personality can excel in whatever career they put their minds to—and you are no exception.

That said, you are definitely best suited for a career that calls for you to use your proverbial noodle. A research position at a university would be appealing—you could literally spend your life learning about any field that fascinates you. You may even consider a career in journalism, through which you could interview interesting people and share your newfound knowledge with the masses.

In the workplace, you are a valuable employee because of your amazing work ethic. You barely get up to take a break, let alone grab coffee, because you're typically so engrossed in the task at hand. People know they can rely on you to take on a project or learn a new skill—once something is in your hands, it will get done and probably better than expected.

Because you're constantly showing others up with your intellectual skills, the people you work with can be a bit icy toward you. And, because you *always* prioritize work over play, you can be a bit of a loner in the office. By coming in early, you can seem a bit of a showoff, and by staying late, you miss happy hours with your colleagues. Loosening up a little will allow you to make friends with those on your team and let them trust you more, not just see you as an overachiever.

YOUR FRIENDSHIPS

Because you tend to get lost in your own research—and your own head—you're a bit of a lone wolf when it comes to friendships in general. You have difficulty making friends sometimes because people don't often understand your desire to always keep learning and your need to put your nose in yet another book.

Another barrier you have when it comes to friendships is ignorance. You find it hard to tolerate people who are closed-minded and not open to new ideas, ways of thinking, and ways of life.

However, finding a similarly geeky friend would be downright amazing; two heads are better than one, after all. You and your brainy BFF could teach each other quite a lot about your differing interests and continually challenge each other to think quicker and be smarter. You two could get lost for hours discussing books, politics, history—you name it!

YOUR LOVE LIFE

As with your friendships, you can have a little bit of a hard time in the love department. You need a partner who shares your passion for learning, is open to new ideas, and totally understands your need to hole up with your laptop pretty much every day for hours on end.

Because you tend to intellectualize everything—even finding a significant other—online dating is a great option for you to find that special someone. You like the idea of an algorithm matching you up with potential suitors, and having your personality define your compatibility rather than your looks.

In a relationship, you are a great partner because you treat your main squeeze like new territory to discover. You're constantly curious about your boyfriend, wanting to understand what makes him tick. Though, when you think you've learned all there is to know about your partner, you tend to get bored, and may even want to move on to someone new . . . so watch out for that!

Your biggest relationship deal breaker is when your partner withholds information—you value honesty and trust, so if your partner lies by omission or keeps something from you, it won't go over well.

YOUR FAMILY LIFE

Growing up, your mom and dad probably valued reading books, watching educational TV, and talking about interesting subjects around the dinner table, and these tenets shaped you into the person you are today.

You look up to your parents for instilling these values in you. However, because knowledge was so important in your household, you did have a bit of a rivalry with your siblings as far as who read the most challenging book or made the most interesting project in school—each of you wanted to impress your parents the most, which likely bred some resentment among your clan.

For you, extended family provides another avenue for knowledge. You're very close to your grandparents and relish the chance to pick their brains about what life was like in their youth. You very much appreciate their stories and wisdom, believing firmly that, like a fine wine, the brain only gets better with age.

Aha! So you don't seem to exactly fit in one faction, eh? Well, while Divergence is something you would need to hide within the realm of the Divergent universe, your secret is safe in our world—in fact, it doesn't need to be a secret at all.

Being Divergent might suggest that you're a little different, but it also means that you have some very interesting possibilities as far as your life is concerned. Read on to learn what your Divergence means for you in the real world.

A FEW OF YOUR FAVORITE THINGS

Color: Green

Role model: Jack Kerouac

Movie or TV show: Freaks and Geeks

Guilty pleasure: Spying on other people to try to understand them

Room in your house: The backyard, where you feel free

Holiday: New Year's Day (each year is a chance to start anew)

Possession: Your family tree

YOUR PERSONALITY

THE UPSIDE

Rather than seeing things in black and white, you tend to see the world—and the situations you encounter within it—in shades of gray. You spend a lot of time running over potential outcomes of your actions in your head, calculating your decisions and weighing options carefully. This is not to say that you're always cautious, but you do instinctively consider who you are, what you should do, and what might happen as a result of your actions.

You wonder, however, if everyone else is like you in this sense and the answer is most likely no. Being Divergent makes you a bit of an outlier, which means that the answers to life's big questions, and even your values and morals, aren't easily defined the way they are for most people.

THE DOWNSIDE

You're often conflicted as far as your values and actions are concerned. You don't quite know when to be honest and when to keep the truth to yourself. You wonder sometimes if a white lie is necessary to spare a person's feelings, which is most typical of people who show an affinity for both Amity and Candor. You struggle to understand when you should put your own self-interests and self-preservation first and when you should be selfless, which is common in people who are split between Erudite and Abnegation. You wonder why you can be so fearful at times, even if you selected many Dauntless-themed answers on your Aptitude Test. You're constantly trying to understand where you fit in, since your emotions do not follow one set track, but seem to be on an ever-shifting spectrum.

YOUR STYLE

In the Divergent universe, where each faction has its own prescribed fashion and attire, the Divergent, in an effort to remain hidden and blend in, pick a faction and follow whatever its inhabitants wear. Otherwise, they risk being labeled Divergent and ending up factionless.

In the real world, you likely still feel on the outskirts of the rest of the people you know, a bit of a loner or misfit. And rather than trying to blend in by following the latest fads, you wear what feels true to you, whether it's jeans and a sweater, or leggings and a crop top. Your style can vary year by year or week by week—you sometimes decide to reinvent yourself (and your look) based on how you're feeling or who you want to be. You use your clothes, hair, and makeup as a way to figure yourself out.

YOUR ACTIVITIES AND HOBBIES

Depending on your Divergent blend, you may have a predisposition toward a love of watching the arts (Amity), or for playing more extreme sports (Dauntless), or for rooting for people in extreme arts competitions (Amity and Dauntless), à la *American Idol*. This is just an example of how your Divergence may play out in your extracurricular life.

You spend a lot of time immersing yourself in your own history, reading journals left by your ancestors and tracing your family tree. You're very interested in your connection to the world and how you got to be who (and how) you are. Finding old letters from your grandparents or a photograph of a long-lost aunt is like a treasure to you, another piece of your puzzle.

To clear your head, you enjoy running, biking, and swimming—solo sports that are non-competitive and simply exist for you to challenge your own body, free of others' influence and judgment.

YOUR WORK LIFE

Because your faction doesn't dictate a predisposition toward one type of career, you have limitless choices as far as work is concerned. Depending on your faction blend, however, you may have a stronger connection with certain niche professions. If you are Candor and Erudite, for example, you might be well suited to create computer simulated lie detector tests or smartphone apps that would help others know when those around them are not telling the truth. If you are Dauntless and Abnegation, you might be an excellent counselor to troubled youth or reformed criminals—you'd be intimidating enough to be just the right amount of scary, but selfless, too.

In the workplace, your faction blend again reveals your true nature. Those with Erudite and Abnegation traits, for example, might be whip-smart and hardworking, but humble about their intelligence or even prone to downplaying their abilities. Those with Dauntless and Amity (a rare combination) may be sweet and unintimidating on the outside but able to strike when a situation calls for them to stand up for themselves or defend someone else.

However, because your emotions can be at odds with one another, you don't typically feel like your actions and feelings are always cut and dry. For the most part, you put your head down, work hard, and hope that your efforts show that you are a valuable member of the team.

YOUR FRIENDSHIPS

Because you can often feel out of place, you may not have a ton of close friends. In fact, you sometimes have a hard time trusting people. Your own mind is such a swirling vortex of conflicting emotion that you assume everyone else would probably think you're crazy if you let them in.

What you don't realize, however, is that even those placed neatly in one faction still struggle with the same issues of love, acceptance, and fear, albeit some more than others. Therefore, sharing your struggles and revealing yourself to others will make people drop their own guards and feel free to express themselves, too.

Being Divergent, the greatest gift you have as a friend is an ability to understand more than one faction's mindset. Because you can comprehend what it means to be selfless, but also honest, or courageous, or kind, you experience a great range of human emotion. You can't be confined to one path of thinking and reasoning—and this is a great asset to those around you who may need a little help seeing multiple sides of a situation.

YOUR LOVE LIFE

Like in friendship, your love life can be a little problematic because you're so guarded. As a misfit, you can come off as being too cool for school (the opposite of how you often feel), which keeps many potential suitors intimidated . . . and too scared to ask you out. By lowering your guard and realizing that the right person will love you for you—no matter how complicated you are—you'll find that ideal partner who will help you take on the world.

You'd be particularly compatible with a fellow Divergent because you could explore the complexities of your faction combinations, having intense discussions about life, your values, and your role in the world.

YOUR FAMILY LIFE

To try to understand who you are and why you are the way you are, you often looked to your parents for clues as you were growing up. You wanted insight not only into your own personality, but how you were to behave responsibly and authentically as an adult.

It wasn't always easy because, even early on, you were able to see flaws in your own parents—you didn't always agree with the way they smoothed out potential arguments without actually talking it out (if your parents were Amity) or spent so much time helping others that they neglected themselves (if they were Abnegation).

Still, they helped you learn how you wanted to be when you grew up and helped shape the vision of the life you wanted to lead. And while they likely knew all along that you were Divergent, they never let that change their love for you or how they treated you.

AFTERWORD

Now that your Aptitude Test is complete and your ideal faction—or Divergence—has been revealed, it's time to put your newfound knowledge to use. No matter which faction you found yourself in after your Aptitude Test, you won't have to make a lifelong decision regarding which one to pick in your Choosing Ceremony. Rather, you can use your newfound knowledge to your advantage—and the betterment of our current world.

Perhaps you belong in Abnegation and your selfless spirit deserves to fly. Consider representing your faction by throwing a charity drive or joining a non-profit. Or simply try chatting up one of your classmates who doesn't seem to have many friends, and encourage him or her to sit with you at lunch. Even a small gesture of generosity means so much to the people on the receiving end.

If Amity is your chosen faction, spread that kindness far and wide. Be the person who tries to make peace the next time your friends get into a squabble. Or take a bigger approach to diplomacy by starting a letter writing campaign for a worldly cause that means a great deal to you.

You may have discovered that you fit best with Candor, and have a strong penchant for telling the truth. Join your school's debate team, if you haven't already, and allow your argumentative skills to shine. Maybe just commit to telling one hard truth a day, choosing an instance in which you might normally fudge things or dance around the facts to just come right out with it.

Did Dauntless choose you? Exercise that fearlessness and stand up for someone, whether a person at school or a group of people needing your assistance. And maybe take your love of an adrenaline rush seriously by checking out an indoor rock-climbing center or taking trapeze lessons.

Maybe Erudite is your faction. Since you're already a book lover (one has to assume), it may be time to pen a tome of your own. Or it could be fun to start a club of fellow intellectuals with whom you could discuss books, ideas, or new inventions. The world will look forward to whatever it is you create when you put your heads together.

And for you Divergent result-getters: Don't fear your out-of-the-box status—embrace it! You cannot be labeled, and therefore your possibilities are endless. Find what truly speaks to you, harness it, and you will succeed.

Whatever faction you fit with, hopefully you now have an interesting perspective on who you are and what matters to you. At the very least, now you know what choice to make if you are suddenly transported into the Divergent universe. Hey, weirder things have happened, right?